veal

the rise of generation interactive

breeding a new consumer class

patrick aievoli

Zea Books, Lincoln, Nebraska • 2016

Copyright © 2016 Patrick Aievoli.

ISBN 978-1-60962-104-9

http://doi.org/10.13014/K2KW5CXV

Zea Books are published by the University of Nebraska–Lincoln Libraries
Electronic (pdf) edition available online at http://digitalcommons.unl.edu
Print edition available from http://www.lulu.com/spotlight/unlib

UNL does not discriminate based upon any protected status.
Please go to unl.edu/nondiscrimination

This book is dedicated to:

Adele, Philip and Allison
and Patsy, Josephine and Andrea

a special thanks to
Magdalena "Maggie" McCormick for her help

and immeasurable thanks to
Dr. Joan Digby and Snowball

Contents

"This instrument can teach, it can illuminate; yes, and even it can inspire. But it can do so only to the extent that humans are determined to use it to those ends. Otherwise, it's nothing but wires and lights in a box. There is a great and perhaps decisive battle to be fought against ignorance, intolerance and indifference. This weapon of television [the Internet] could be useful."

– Edward R. Murrow

http://www.rtdna.org/content/edward_r_murrow_s_1958_wires_lights_in_a_box_speech#sthash.ChdJjzG0.dpuf

Preface

The purpose of this book is to investigate and discuss the premise that the current generation was constructed to be consumers for a transitional marketplace.

As the economy shifted from analog to digital, consumers had to be trained to accept, use and progress within a new economic model through changes in societal and economic patterns. During the course of this book those patterns will be discussed and displayed as a confluence of:

- Marketplace manipulation

- Abusive use of technologies

- Lack of governance

In this book I will discuss how those events are reflected in the habits and lifestyles of the current 12 to 25 year old demographic globally and how it has caused them to be the consummate consumer of digital goods based on events that have been created to develop them to be consumers and to be consumed. One of the first questions is whether this was the fault of parenting; in my opinion – no, it was more the position families were placed in and how they best could survive. When many events come into play and seemingly conspire to force families to re-invent themselves, it is not so much the fault of the "herd" but the result of the "rancher".

But why is this important to anyone and what gives me the right to discuss this?

A quick, poignant synopsis of this book -

"Veal: the rise of generation interactive" is a deft manifesto on the domestication of the young consumer into a well-cultivated piece of "veal" ready to be parceled off to greedy corporations as a permanent food source, while governments either ineptly, or corruptly, look the other way.

Pat Aievoli's "Veal" has a Chomsky-esque mix of cynicism (the system) and genuine optimism (parents and teachers nobly struggling to keep up), infused with an edgy Mike Ruppert-esque assertion of conspiracy and determination to have his "Voice from the Wilderness" ... of Academia, heard. He sees the confluence of events in the 1980's-2000s (technological advances, lifestyle trends in families, the rise of maladies such as ADD, ADHD, and autism, and market manipulations and crashes) lead to a new digital economy that was premeditated on a global scale to become overbearingly extractive, and an educational system that is less savvy than the students, to the point students have disengaged out of boredom. He sees that combination resulting in predatory "educational" corporations that come and go, razing and "re-teching" our instructional practices and institutions, as frequent and relentless plagues of locusts. He attempts to examine causality, as a means to a remedy, or, at least, awareness – the first step toward any solution. Chock full of pop-culture and contemporaneous references, interesting statistics, and quotes from humanity's deep thinkers, this is a fascinating must-read for educators and administrators, as well as consumers, parents, and students.

— Kristine O'Malley-Levy, Former Board member of Mensa of Greater New York, and Educator

Foreword

To answer those questions from the preface we need to look at economic markets to see if they are true and change naturally through a free market system or if they are manipulated to intertwine and work together to the detriment of society – specifically the current 12 to 25 year olds?

- Have markets been manipulated today more than ever?
- What is the new economy and is growth totally "digital"?
- Has any effort been made to stop these events?

These questions raise further questions, but we need to have the facts first. So to that end I have used very generous portions of research materials. This was done to give a very fair and objective viewpoint to the reader. In a recent interview between comedians David Steinberg and Stephen Colbert, Steinberg asked Colbert why his joke setups were so long? To paraphrase his answer: "I needed to get everyone on the same page or the joke wouldn't work." My belief is the same, in order to literally and figuratively get everyone on the same page for my readers to get my point I have tried to not edit the research to be favorable or prejudiced. Therefore allowing them to disagree or agree with the logic presented in the following questions.

Has the price of the housing market been manipulated to make the two-income family a necessity? Has the basis of the economy shifted to a "digital marketplace"? Has there been any manipulation of laws to allow this to happen?

Usually most free market pricing is based on supply and demand. The only time the population of the United States grew substantially was during the "Baby Boom" era. But even then, housing prices were affordable and a one-income family was sufficient. What happened and why?

In developed nations globally – the new economic models are being driven by the consumption of a digital product base from a younger and younger age group - is this really true? Well ask yourself if you believe adults age 25 and over consume as much digital product as that 12-25 demographic – and even younger ones?

Why were laws like "Glass-Steagall" overturned right before a huge housing market crash?

"This repeal was arguably one of the largest deregulation bills of the financial services industry in U.S. history. Essentially, it reversed Glass Steagall and allowed members of the financial services industry to enter each others' businesses."

http://www.usc.edu/org/InsightBusiness/ib/articles/articlescontent/08_4%20Adrianna%20Smith.html

And why has Net Neutrality - the ownership of the Internet - become such a "hot potato"?

Have other developed countries allowed their next generation to become prey to this new economy?

Why me?

Who am I that I have a perspective on this phenomenon? For the last 30 years I have been — as a designer/developer and teacher — involved in the evolution of interaction design. In the 1980's I was a distant part of the team that created some of the first CD-ROMs used in educational publishing. Over that time I received a Masters in Multimedia Design and have worked on some of the most well known corporate endeavors into this space. I have also taught this discipline (full time) at the college level for 28 of those years and I believe I am personally responsible for many careers that have designed and developed products that you use every day, from shopping online to reviewing your healthcare status. This new economy is dependent on a sophisticated user. As Jef Raskin (Apple developer) said, "As far as the customer is concerned, the interface is the product."

Why is it important to understand what and how it happened?

First of all, these changes directly affect our children, and usually nothing is more important to our lives than them. Secondly, Their futures as citizens should be our main concern even if we have no children of our own.

But what are we talking about here? The focus is on their well-being and futures and how possibly an opportunistic or required change in economies desperately needed a new consumer.

Have those changes come together in a "perfect storm" by chance? My belief is that they were constructed to become a "perfect storm" and not just an opportunity to be grabbed. I believe in Ockham's Razor which states that, "among competing hypotheses, the one with the fewest assumptions should be selected."

The following chapters attempt to construct that hypothesis, but based I believe on the most complete version of the research possible.

Chapter 1
Scaring the "herd"

What were the pieces of this "perfect storm"?

Nothing scares people more than the inability to provide basic care for themselves or their loved ones. And that starts with providing shelter from the storm. What were the pieces of this "perfect storm"?

Basic Necessities

For the first time in the history of this country housing prices responded far further than market demand. And in response to that surge in prices a two-income family was necessary for most households. Even during the baby boom marketplace housing prices were affordable enough to maintain a one-income family structure. Since 1980 it was deemed a luxury for the family to have just one income, thus necessitating a non-traditional process for child rearing. In other developed nations, this has been compensated by parental leave, healthcare, vacation time, etc. Was this market manipulation made possible by the repeal of the Glass-Steagall act – a law that prohibited the banks and investment companies from merging funds?

At the same time during the 1980s the rise of the home entertainment, game console and personal computers occurred - a venture with great possibly positive outcomes, but used primarily by many as indoctrination to habits, that at the same time coupled with a lack of supervision contributed to a dramatic rise in obesity (sugar based diet) and a diagnosis of ADD and ADHD.

During and prior to this "perfect storm" housing prices became the target of many unscrupulous groups – not our traditional criminal types arguably – but what was our governing body. And the battle over the ownership of the delivery vehicle – the Internet known as "Net Neutrality" has been fought and lost.

In discussion with people while writing this book, I have found that some discounted the concept of a "conspiracy-like" happening, well here is a simple definition –

Simple Definition of conspiracy

> *: a secret plan made by two or more people to do something that is harmful or illegal*
>
> *: the act of secretly planning to do something that is harmful or illegal*

http://www.merriam-webster.com/dictionary/conspiracy

So let's ask the question, does what happened in the 1980s and recently in 2000's fit that definition? To answer that question we will review the research on the timing of repealing the Glass-Steagall Act and articles on the "Keating 5" and "The Big Short."

How did this "perfect storm" create a new economy? How did it affect our educational and societal models? How did all of these ripples affect our children – physically, mentally, socially and educationally - specifically the lack of technology in the classroom and how the children of "generation interactive or gen-i" became frustrated with traditional teaching methods and practices to the point of intolerance and malaise? How much of this is the fault of educators and the educational system?

Right or wrong you need to speak to the student's experience-

> *"If we teach today's students as we taught yesterday's, we rob them of tomorrow."* — *John Dewey*

Are we – as "digital immigrants" - not speaking to these students in their – "digital native" – language and therefore are we causing the conversation to be one-sided. This is just one line item in a much bigger list of issues but one that can be remedied. Have they been pre-programmed to respond only to certain stimuli? Are we not fluent enough in that language thus creating too much distance between the generations? Did we have enough time to assimilate these changes or has the speed been too fast and the time too short? So they tune out the same way many in the majority age group and ethnicity tune out when Selma Hayek or Javier Bardem accepts an award and speaks in fluent Spanish. We nod and say isn't he or she beautiful and never care to understand what she is saying. They just nod and think about something else – usually with no response. This has always been the case in school, even in college, but today there seems to be a flip of the 80/20 break down. For years 80% paid attention at least somewhat with 20% lost in the ozone, but today it seems that that has flipped to 20% paying attention and the 80% being immersed in distraction and just general malaise. We will discuss what I and others feel is the cause of this in later chapters.

A fellow educator and I had the same analogy – strangely at different times. We both said that the current lack of familiarity that educators have with social media creates a void in prescribing sustenances similar to bringing children to an exotic food store but not explaining how nutrition works and allowing them to just eat whatever they want. We are feeding them but allowing them to just grab whatever it is they want. We need to learn the store, but it is much more difficult than usual because they already know the store and our ignorance invalidates our credibility to govern their choices. So in avoiding learning about the store we give an even greater validity to our lack of credibility.

I am a parent to two children who fit snuggly into that 12-25 year old demographic. So I have witnessed this from the outside and the inside while always trying to do good work while balancing the possibility of addiction and demise of current qualities of life as best I could with my dual responsibilities. And has the battle over Net Neutrality occurred primarily to control the delivery vehicle for this new digital marketplace?

In this book I will be presenting facts and trying to use those facts to create a scenario that accounts for this new "veal" generation. Why is the "how" important – well so obviously we can be vigilant to stop it from progressing further. And to also know what predatory practices like the late night educational infomercial remedies are real or fraudulent. How many learning center or educational product commercials have you seen to help Johnny or Lexi learn to read or do math better? How many proposed plans for better educational initiatives have you read about or voted on at your school board? But yet nothing seems to work. Common Core initiatives – yikes – will go on for years and years, ruining generation after generation as the ed. tech pirates sweep in and pillage the district.

The goal here is to try and see how this all happened? Why and how were the markets manipulated? How does something like Flint, Michigan's lead in the water happen? Where have our tax dollars been going all these years? Is this just a full swing of the pendulum or has the ability to see deeper via better transparency – again by the use of social media allowed for this to be unveiled? What are the signals/routes to stop it and to turn it all around?

Why "veal?"

Many of my friends, colleagues and family hate that I have named this book – "veal". They have asked me to change it because they find the analogy rude and offensive. Good – now that I have your attention let's talk it out. I have been in advertising since 1976, and one thing I learned if you want to cut through the clutter and get to the core of your message – keep it simple and minimal – and one word usually does that.

Jerry Della-Famina (a very famous adman from the 1960s and on) has a story of when a Jewish cemetery group wanted a new campaign. Supposedly when the presentation day came around he unveiled his new slogan for them – "Plotz!" In

Yiddish it means to drop dead instantly. I don't think he got the account but he did get their attention.

Quickly gaining your attention was one of the first goals but also it is to establish again who is who?

Obviously the "veal" is the new generation of consumers. And the "herd" is the society from where it was conceived originally. But the one part that seems to keep getting misunderstood is the "rancher". Who is the entity that is controlling this process – the "rancher?" Well in most cases of rearing livestock the "rancher" is the one making the immediate decisions based on the "marketplace". So to that end the "rancher", in this metaphor is being directly influenced by the three forces outlined before in the forward.

- Marketplace manipulation
- Abusive use of technologies
- Lack of governance

Now did these three forces work in perfect concert? Who knows; but, when this many things come together so seamlessly one has to question. Something so simple to do like getting clean water to certain parts of this country can't happen but somehow all of these complex things just happened by sheer chance?

Is getting your attention and bringing all of us out of the haze of the Kardashians and Reality Television just part of the goal? Getting you to take a step back and ask, "What is actually going on here?" That is the goal of the title, and hopefully it will be substantiated throughout this book.

So why pick the name "veal?" Why use the term "veal"? Because veal by definition is: a young cow that has been purposely raised in a manner to create a specific end product. The calf had many other outcomes but the rancher purposely engaged a process for a specific result. Just to be clear here again – the "rancher" is not the parents. It is the CEOs responding to the societal governing body that allowed this to happen through the confluence of laws and practices. These ranchers order other associates like mortgage lenders, software developers, and local politicians to follow their lead.

The parents are the older cattle part of the "herd" (which created the calf), they are responsible to a degree. But, you can't blame someone for not tap dancing well when you keep tying their shoelaces together.

What is veal?

Veal is meat from young calves, slaughtered when they are about six months old. In many countries, including the UK, veal is bound up with milk production and mostly comes from bull calves born to dairy cows. Organic farmer Helen Browning of Eastbrook Farm, one of the few farmers producing and selling high-welfare British veal says, 'if you drink milk you have a responsibility to think about what happens to the male calves'.

Milking cows are separated from their calves after giving birth and made to continue lactating. Female calves can become milkers, but the herd does not need males and dairy breeds are not ideally suited to rearing for beef. So redundant calves can be kept with the herd for a few months and then killed for veal.

But with no market for veal our dairy farmers still have to dispose of the unwanted calves. The choice is horrific: either shoot them when they're a few days old, or condemn them to a horrendous fate by exporting them to Europe, where veal production thrives. There they will be reared in conditions that are illegal in the UK.

http://www.bbc.co.uk/food/food_matters/veal.shtml

Veal crating is criticized because the ability of the calves to move is highly restricted; the crates have unsuitable flooring; the calves spend their entire lives indoors, experience prolonged sensory, social, and exploratory deprivation; and the calves are more susceptible to high amounts of stress and disease.[12] According to the Veal Quality Assurance Program, the Veal Issues Management Program industry fact sheet, and the Ontario Veal Association, individual housing systems are important for disease control and in reducing the possibility of physical injury. Furthermore, they state it also allows for veal farmers to provide more personal attention to veal calves.

http://www.humanesociety.org/farm/resources/research/wel-fare/welfare_veal_calves.html

Below is a simplified list of what creates veal.

- *Born*
- *Separated from mother*
- *Moved elsewhere to be raised*
- *Kept in a small space*
- *Stimulated just enough to create desired end product*
- *Once ready, sold off in pieces and individual prices*

I truly believe that this generation was created as "veal" to consume and be consumed by a new digital economy. The question now is how and why did this happen to this generation? Why was it necessary? What were the steps that were put into place and how does it all relate to creating this new economic model?

Creating an economy

Throughout history economies have usually responded to human need. A need arises and a service or product is then built to fill that need. Simple Supply and Demand – here is it explained for 6th graders, purposely kept simple to insure understanding. Of course there are many variations and growth areas but at the base level it is just simple – you have something and people need it, not just want it.

Supply and Demand: Basic Economics

Part 2: Comparisons on Price

So we have supply, which is how much of something you have, and demand, which is how much of something people want. Put the two together, and you have supply and demand.

Now, how do you show the relationship between the two? One way is to use the price of something. Generally speaking, the price of something will go up if the demand goes up. Why? Because the seller thinks he or she can get more money for whatever he or she is selling.

If more people want something, they will be willing to pay more for it. A good example is the newest basketball shoes. Everybody wants them, and they will be willing to pay more than they normally would to get them. The demand goes up. Why? Because more people want them. The price also goes up. Why? Because the seller knows he or she can get more money for the product because it is in demand.

In the same way, the price will go down when the demand goes down. When the new style of basketball shoes comes out, everyone wants the new shoes. The old shoes don't seem so new anymore. The seller still wants to sell those older shoes, since he or she has a lot still in stock. So, the price goes down. Why? The seller hopes that people will be willing to buy the older shoes at a lower price. After all, the older shoes aren't that much older or worse than the brand new shoes.

http://www.socialstudiesforkids.com/articles/economics/supplyanddemand2.htm

But what happens when the market completely changes? What happens when the market is destroyed? An example is the advent of the automobile. Horses gave way to cars to travel expediently, and then the gasoline market became relevant. Before that gasoline was considered a "throw-a-way" from the oil production process.

> "Gasoline was around before the invention of the internal combustion engine but for many years was considered a useless by-product of the refining of crude oil to make kerosene, a standard fuel for lamps through much of the 19th century."

> http://www.greatachievements.org/?id=3677

It was thought to be of no value. Imagine gasoline – the substance that literally and figuratively drives our economy thought to have no value? We will discuss the effect of these changes later via Joseph Schumpeter's model of Creative Destruction.

My belief, and the purpose of this book, is to demonstrate that for the first time in history a consumer was scientifically and consciously bred for the sole purpose of being a consumer who would support and drive a new environment – one in which all previous processes have almost no relevance, an economy with no need for store shelves, clerks, salespeople, local warehouse workers or packaging.

How would an existing generation of purchasers, who were used to holding an object, find something that they could not physically hold worth their money - would they embrace it?

Understand, we have always had a service product economic model – life insurance – retirement products – but even within something as ephemeral as the arts we could hold the album, the painting, the film, the video. We had something to point to and say there is my money's worth on that shelf, or that wall - there is what I bought.

In class I have referenced Walter Benjamin's "Art in the Age of Mechanical Reproduction" to speak to a digital product, using the discussion of replication and value, but now how do we validate the actual digital? How would an existing generation with all of the purchasing power help fuel a new economic model that is intangible? Would that generation see any validity in purchasing something that as has been called "ten thousand songs that fit in your jean's pocket"? This is a hard proof of concept and one that, in my opinion could have died on the vine. No pun intended. So a new generation had to be created.

Many industries have had a very tough time accepting this new model and many would fall away under this process. Once you read Schumpeter's Creative Destruction theory you will see how this evolutionary process has gone on for decades. Those that did not evolve would simply close shop and disappear – think horsewhips and cars.

Today you scroll through a playlist and amass followers for a product. You point to Google analytics or Facebook "likes" to measure worth. How was this going to translate into value from the basis of an analogue economic base? When or has this ever happened before? Think "Pet Rock" or any fad – usually short time-frames and minimal value. Rarely, if ever has an entire country's economy been dependent on a fad or non-existent commodity.

Recently HBO aired a documentary on Jerry Weintraub. In the documentary Weintraub recounts a meeting with his father, who came out to visit his very successful son, now an entertainment producer living in Los Angeles. According to his obituary in the New York Times -

> *"Jerry Weintraub, a consummate showman whose up-and-down career touched musical entertainers as grandly diverse as Elvis Presley, Frank Sinatra and Led Zeppelin and screen artists who included Steven Soderbergh, Robert Altman and Michael Douglas, died on Monday in Santa Barbara, Calif. He was 77."*
> http://www.nytimes.com/2015/07/07/arts/jerry-weintraub-a-force-in-film-and-music-dies-at-77.html

The senior Weintraub was a jewelry salesman from Brooklyn who would concoct wild stories about his products to create buzz or basically what we call today social media marketing. In the meeting between the father and son the elder asked the son "where is your inventory?" – the father was looking for physical items. Weintraub the son states in the documentary that he just pointed to his head and said, "it is all up here."

This is a great example of the product being stored in a cloud and used on demand and never being able to go out of stock, basically the ultimate computer storage system and one that is referred to as the (Alan) Turing test - measuring a computer's speed of calculation against the human brain. Weintraub was setting the benchmark for that test in the media and entertainment field obviously others would do it in their respective fields but Weintraub's portfolio of work had the greatest mass appeal reaching millions upon millions of "users." But it wasn't an entire country's economy and it didn't change value across the globe. Let's look at when that did happen because this book is about challenging the premise of our current digital world and what had to happen to redirect a global economy from a very personal and pedestrian perspective.

As an example let's look at the earliest recorded occurrence of a fad-like economy – but again physical. In the mid 1600s Holland experienced what has come to be called "The Tulip Bubble" -

History of the Tulip Bubble

"Tulpenwoede" (tulip madness) resulted in big increases in tu-lip prices. At the beginning of 1637, some tulip contracts reached a level about 20 times the level of three months earlier. A partic-ularly rare tulip, Semper Augustus, was priced at around 1,000 guilders in the 1620's. But just before the crash, it was valued at 5,500 guilders per bulb—roughly the cost of a luxurious house in Amsterdam. Prices collapsed in February 1637—although data here are particularly poor—and a few investors left bankrupt.

The price swings were not caused by massive changes to pro-duction costs. Nor did tulips suddenly become particularly useful. As a result, most people assume that tulipmania was the result of financial market irrationality. That idea was popularized by Charles Mackay, a mid-19th century Scottish writer. Most modern-day references to tulipmania draw on Mackay's work. But, eco-nomic historians provide better explanations for what happened.

Earl Thompson, formerly of UCLA, takes a different approach. He reckons that the market for tulips was an efficient response to changing financial regulation—in particular, the anticipated gov-ernment conversion of futures contracts into options contracts. This ruse was dreamt up by government officials, who themselves were keen to make a quick buck from the tulip trade.

In plain English, investors who had bought the right to buy tu-lips in the future were no longer obliged to buy them. If the mar-ket price was not high enough for investors' liking, they could pay a small fine and cancel the contract. The balance between risk and reward in the tulip market was skewed massively in in-vestors' favour. The inevitable result was a huge increase in tulip options prices (see below right). (The price of options collapsed when the government saw sense and cancelled the contracts.) Spot prices (the price that traders paid for immediate delivery of tulips) and futures prices (the prices that traders would be com-pelled to pay for future delivery of tulips) were not volatile. And any movement of the spot/futures price was determined by simple supply and demand—the fall-out from the Thirty Years' War, one of the bloodiest in European history, was one important factor. http://www.economist.com/blogs/freeexchange/2013/10/ economic-history

Well it does seem like war is the great reset button for any economic progres-sion. If we have no economy we have a war – think Great Depression to World

War II to the prosperous 1950s. Think about how once the Military Industrial Complex was setup at the end of World War II how it was then exercised in the Korean War just enough to test it out. Then once we knew how the pieces worked we had Vietnam, the never-ending war that finally got resolved once Nixon/Kissinger opened the gates to trade with China. Now think how once the "Dot com" boom got really rolling downhill how that was quickly stopped by 9/11. Economies drive countries, and conflict between countries drive economics and once that economy was challenged by a new economic model that had very little to do with the previous structure, the pudding really hit the blender.

So here are my questions. Are all economic trends based on need or want? When one is destroyed does the next one go forward via a new model or simply restart on the same premise with a new name, story, new government regulations and deregulations?

Are regulations ever benevolent or always predatory? Has any economic model actually needed to create their customers before? One of the theories that I personally find extremely relevant is that of Joseph Schumpeter – Creative Destruction.

Schumpeter's Model

Let me offer a simple explanation using a few lay citations.

> *Joseph Schumpeter (1883–1950) coined the seemingly paradoxical term "creative destruction," and generations of economists have adopted it as a shorthand description of the free market's messy way of delivering progress. In Capitalism, Socialism, and Democracy (1942), the Austrian economist wrote:*

> *The opening up of new markets, foreign or domestic, and the organizational development from the craft shop to such concerns as U.S. Steel illustrate the same process of industrial mutation—if I may use that biological term—that incessantly revolutionizes the economic structure from within, incessantly destroying the old one, incessantly creating a new one. This process of Creative Destruction is the essential fact about capitalism. (p. 83)*

More from the same article which points towards the problem and how the companies seeing their own demise may have reviewed the process and tried to make sure they themselves didn't fall off the cliff.

> *Over the past two centuries, the Western nations that embraced capitalism have achieved tremendous economic progress as new industries supplanted old ones. Even with the higher living*

standards, however, the constant flux of free enterprise is not always welcome. The disruption of lost jobs and shuttered businesses is immediate, while the payoff from creative destruction comes mainly in the long term. As a result, societies will always be tempted to block the process of creative destruction, implementing policies to resist economic change.

And to me the biggest and truest point made in this article.

Attempts to save jobs almost always backfire. Instead of going out of business, inefficient producers hang on, at a high cost to consumers or taxpayers. The tinkering short-circuits market signals that shift resource to emerging industries. It saps the incentives to introduce new products and production methods, leading to stagnation, layoffs, and bankruptcies. The ironic point of Schumpeter's iconic phrase is this: societies that try to reap the gain of creative destruction without the pain find themselves enduring the pain but not the gain.

http://www.pewinternet.org/2012/04/17/ the-future-of-money-in-a-mobile-age-2/

http://www.econlib.org/library/Enc/CreativeDestruction.html

How is this working today?

Given the previous years' unemployment rates at nearly double digits and the lack of upward mobility for the current generation, why has this part of Schumpeter's Theory seemed to have been adopted by so many companies? Why is the transition to a digital product so slow? Just look at GE's new ad campaign featuring coding as the new product line over the behemoth-like physical products of their past.

My belief (from 30 years of observation) is because the right consumer was not in a buying power position. They had to be bred; for even just growing up with an old mindset would not be enough to guarantee success of this new digital economic model.

Most media and product or companies have leveraged loans based on actual dollar profits, so even if you moved 1000 units and they were digital you didn't make the same dollar amount as an analogue model – iTunes model versus CD model. The actual profit margin (in percentages) is much higher but the actual dollars on the profit statement were lower. This triggered all sorts of problems like higher business loan rates and lower stock prices; which then required a greater profit margin in respect to dollars spent, typically in reducing labor costs.

So more hours for less pay – to me – would be a formula, that led to the stagnation in wages we have witnessed for the last decade.

This is why there is such a great divide between the rich and poor today – probably wider (according to Reich's bridge chart) than has been in the last 100 years? Causing society to go backwards towards a 1% - 99% economic model – witnessed last only prior to the Great Depression of 1929. Was it done for a re-ordering of the economic landscape based on the need for growth in third-world countries to first-world status? And is that needed while the first-world switched from a base of raw materials economy to refined digital products by using individuals as the raw materials? Remember the quote concerning how important the user is in the mix –

> *"In 2015 Uber, the world's largest taxi-company owns no vehicles, Facebook the world's most popular media owner creates no content, Alibaba, the most valuable retailer has no inventory and Airbnb the world's largest accommodation provider owns no real estate."*

This is evident today and it is growing not receding. Why is this important to a designer? Well again to quote Jef Raskin – "The interface is the product."

So today, Interaction Design and those team members - UX (User Experience) designers and the lot are a driving force behind the new economic model. They design interfaces solely for use in a digital space. This career area has seen unprecedented growth in the last few years, with diverse career opportunities clearly outlined as in the diagram below.

(User Experience is a team effort)

In any economic model we need to establish the raw materials and the production base. In this model one of the main components in that scenario is the user. The coding can be done, the devices can be made, the products can be shipped, the bills can be paid, but none of this will happen without a compliant and sophisticated user. And since the current user a generation ago didn't have the sophistication, one had to be built.

For example, look at the profits of two totally different economic models – analogue and digital. One company relies upon the extremely complex process of refining extinct carbon based life forms and the other allows for users to catapult imaginary "birds" at other imaginary objects. Just look at the numbers -

ExxonMobil Earns $32.5 Billion in 2014 –

http://www.forbes.com/sites/maggiemcgrath/2014/07/31/exxon-mobil-and-conocophillips-in-negative-stock-territory-despite-profit-growth/

Apple has recorded the biggest annual profit in corporate history, with record sales of the iPhone helping it to make $53.4bn (£35bn) in the last 12 months – (2014)

http://www.telegraph.co.uk/technology/apple/11959016/Apple-reports-biggest-annual-profit-in-history.html

Again why is this within the purview of a designer? Remember - "the interface is the product" – this has never been truer than today. The new economy is digital and growing. Just in 2015 the Christmas season showed a 2.9% rise in brick and mortar sales versus over 20% rise in online sales – CBS news. So who is doing this purchasing? Is it because the "Gen-i" group has now hit the real purchasing level and why now?

The next section hopes to answer these questions.

Chapter 2
Born
Second baby-boom?

In the years from 1947 to 1964 the United States experienced the largest growth in birth rates since the 1900s.

> *The overall U.S. birth rate peaked most recently in the Baby Boom years, reaching 122.7 in 1957, nearly double today's rate. The birth rate sagged through the mid-1970's but stabilized at 65-70 births per 1,000 women for most years after that before falling again after 2007, the beginning of the Great Recession.* –
>
> *http://www.pewsocialtrends.org/2012/11/29/u-s-birth-rate-falls-to-a-record-low-decline-is-greatest-among-immigrants/*

But since that time the rate dropped and stayed at that new consistent rate until 1990. Then you can see a short burst of growth and then a plateau. You will also notice that there is pretty much a flat-line from 1970 to 1982. Then surge and drop until 1997. Then surge and drop again from 2000 to 2008. No huge spike like the baby boom era. No huge need for housing increases like the era after the war. So now here is the next question – why the huge surge in housing prices at these times. The average home price in 1974 was $39,000.00. Population in the United States in 1974 was 213,853,928.

> *http://www.statisticbrain.com/home-sales-average-price/*
>
> *https://www.census.gov/population/estimates/nation/popclock-est.txt*

Birth Rates, 1920-2010

Births per 1,000 women ages 15-44

Source: Statistics calculated using data obtained from the National Center for Health Statistics and Heuser (1976), available here

PEW RESEARCH CENTER

The population of the United States in 2016 is 322,762,018, a and the average home price is $186,000.00. That is roughly a 500 percent increase, but the population didn't go up by 5 times. So why was there such a spike in home prices from 1974 to 2016?

> http://www.statisticbrain.com/home-sales-average-price/
>
> http://www.usnews.com/opinion/blogs/robert-schlesinger/articles/2016-01-05/us-population-in-2016-according-to-census-estimates-322-762-018

Please see the next chart – a coordinated series of spikes with reference to birth rates – more families means more need for housing which means prices go up whenever something is in demand. So, why the spikes in housing prices in the 1980s and again, in the 2000s if the spikes are not in coordination with the demand?

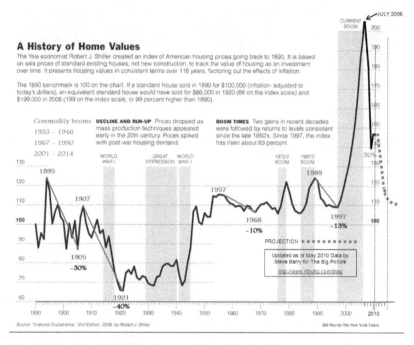

A History of Home Values

The Yale economist Robert J. Shiller created an index of American housing prices going back to 1890. It is based on sale prices of standard existing houses, not new construction, to track the value of housing as an investment over time. It presents housing values in consistent terms over 116 years, factoring out the effects of inflation.

The 1890 benchmark is 100 on the chart. If a standard house sold in 1890 for $100,000 (inflation- adjusted to today's dollars), an equivalent standard house would have sold for $66,000 in 1920 (66 on the index scale) and $199,000 in 2006 (199 on the index scale, or 99 percent higher than 1890).

Commodity booms	DECLINE AND RUN-UP Prices dropped as mass production techniques appeared early in the 20th century. Prices spiked with post-war housing demand.	BOOM TIMES Two gains in recent decades were followed by returns to levels consistent since the late 1950's. Since 1997, the index has risen about 83 percent.
1933 - 1946		
1967 - 1980		
2001 - 2014		

Updated as of May 2010 Data by
Steve Barry for The Big Picture
http://www.ritholtz.com/blog

Source: "Irrational Exuberance," 2nd Edition 2006, by Robert J. Shiller

Bill Marsh/The New York Times

Remember the bulleted process of creating veal.

- *Born*
- *Separated from mother*
- *Moved elsewhere to be raised*
- *Kept in a small space*
- *Stimulated just enough to create desired end product*
- *Once ready sold off in pieces and individual prices*

Were the 1980s and the 2003 housing market done purposefully and not just a free market fluctuation? Well "why" and "how" would you do that? The "why" is obvious – to create an opportunity to capitalize on this vulnerability and also to generate huge profits for the lenders.

How do you create a need for extra revenue? You increase the cost of basic necessities to a level where one income will not cover the monthly costs. This is a very simple equation – choose between a very modest lifestyle – what you think is depriving your child's needs or believe you can make up for time lost. We even came up with a term – "quality time" – hell, all my time is quality.

What is the simplest most effective way of creating that necessity? Focus on one main payment that goes to one main source – mortgages and mortgage lenders. This causes the separation between parent and child – mother/father and calf. Many times I have heard that this is placing guilt on working mothers, quite the opposite. Mothers are the backbone behind the family today, in my humble opinion. Often the working mother has to have dual roles – full time job, and full time parent. Just know I came from a family where I had six aunts – and they drove the bus - big time! So no slight to working mothers here just the opposite.

The "how" is determined by who has control over the pricing.Just like the "block busting" tactics of the 1960s. Realtors and lenders work together to start a new norm within the marketplace. The question then of who benefits can be described through this scenario. Just like when a crime is committed the questions of motive and opportunity come up. First establish the crime – the murdering of the American Dream, as numerous families knew it, across the United States.

Next opportunity. Who had the opportunity to raise housing prices and to create a situation where the money was flowing from the pockets of families to the banks in the form of mortgages? The realtors and the banks did – didn't they? You have no job, no credit, not enough savings – not enough of a problem to stop the faucet of free flowing home equity loans and mortgages. This all worked great until it was time to resell or until the jobs that those mortgagees worked at dried up. Just like fattening up a calf before turning it into "veal". Don't take my word for it go read or watch "The Big Short", you'll start to get the message. The great line – "they're all walking around like they're in an Enya video" and "they're just concerned about the game and dancing shows on TV."

Here is a very recent map that shows the necessary income to buy a home in major cities around the United States. I believe these numbers do not include any other costs.

http://www.hsh.com/finance/mortgage/salary-home-buying-25-cities.html

And on the next page put into a chart for better analysis.

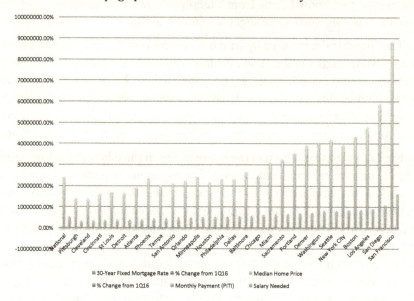

Remember the average salary in the United States according to the Social Security website:

Latest index

The national average wage index for 2014 is 46,481.52. The index is 3.55 percent higher than the index for 2013.

https://www.ssa.gov/oact/cola/AWI.html

In this next chapter we will further discuss the mechanism and the effects of that breakdown of the American Dream as a reality.

Chapter 3
Separating them from the "herd"
Weapons of mass distraction

Throughout this book I have been comparing the construction of this demographic to that of raising "veal." We started with birth, determined the market need for care and housing and now following the comparison further comes the time of separation from the herd.

Did housing prices – mortgages – cause these children to be separated from the herd? Many would think the answer is yes. Just the other day, I had lunch at a small sandwich shop in a strip mall, which had a child-care center down the row. As I was eating my lunch by the window two carts with about eight children riding in them slowly rolled past my view. The attendants wheeled the kids around the parking lot for what I guess was some fresh air. This went on for about 10 minutes, and then they went back inside. This to me was not a normal childhood event. I remember being outside so long in good weather that I got a suntan just from sitting in a carriage.

The need for surrogate parenting has risen dramatically in the last 30 years, in my opinion proportionate to mortgages. As the monthly payment grew so did the need for these centers.

Child-care centers have grown over 300% since 1980. Has this rate been reflected in other areas? I believe in pattern recognition, so let's see.

My first house purchased in 1987 was approximately 3 times the cost of a similar house in 1978. Then when we sold it in 2004 it had grown to 3 times that price. All of this is illustrated by the previous statistics. They call them "bubbles" but are they real or manufactured? Did the increase in cost at 3x's the previous price drive up the use of child-care centers by 3x's? And what effect does this have on families?

How much of an influence has this surrogate parenting had on our children? Were they stimulated or were they just left alone all day? How much was electronic and how much human? How has the child care industry responded in growth to the needs of this new economy?

The number of child care facilities has increased greatly over the last several decades, with <u>U.S. Census Bureau</u> figures showing an increase to 766,401 child care facilities in 2007 from 262,511 facilities in 1987. Demand has been driven by increased numbers of working women, the <u>Census Bureau</u> says. In fact, 61% of mothers with kids under the age of three are working or looking for work, and changes in family structure and the desire to provide young children with educational opportunities have also contributed to demand, according to the government. Nine in 10 child care businesses don't have employees (other than the owner), and these businesses, many of which are operated in-home, require less financial investment than larger centers and therefore, allow owners to readily enter and exit the market as needed.

<u>http://www.forbes.com/sites/sageworks/2014/06/15/ heres-the-growth-chart-on-day-care-businesses/</u>

<u>http://www.huffingtonpost.com/2015/01/20/middle-class- charts_n_6507506.html</u>

Figure One: Median Income and Change in Price of Select Goods 1990-2013
(1990=100)

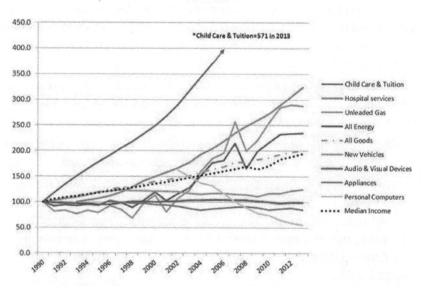

Source: Authors calculations of Bureau of Labor Statistics data (price data for personal computers, hospital services, and appliances were only available beginning in 1993, 2002 and 1996, respectively)

What effect has this had on these children, now that we have had a large portion of a generation who were used to not being told what to do and when to do it simply got older. Some believe that the time in day care is more structured than time at home. But is this time structured for the child or for the child's caregiver?

Many of these children, whether at home or in daycare, were raised by electronic devices and were given free reign over their own time. Statistics show that Americans are working way more than the typical 40-hour week. Email, messaging, computers in general do not leave time for "down time". Even on vacation American workers check their email ten times more than any other worker in the world. So where is the "quality time"? Imagine working a 60-hour week, then you come home and there are typical chores to do, then dinner and how much time is left to parent? So it's time to get plopped in front of the electronics or, worse just left to their own devices (literally) and discretion. Now imagine being a teacher and trying to tell Johnny he has to do what you say to do? We all know how that is working out today. "Baltimore Mom" during the riots in Baltimore over the Freddie Gray incident - was an amazing display of frustration and end game. On the other side of the spectrum was the case of the "Affluenza" teen. He is charged with multiple homicides and the defense was his wealth.

http://www.cnn.com/2015/04/28/us/baltimore-riot-mom-smacks-son/

http://www.cbsnews.com/news/affluenza-teen-ethan-couch-sentenced-to-nearly-two-years-in-jail/

Was this manipulation of an entire generation a coincidence or is it like when land is sold to new home owners and the original owner strips it of all natural resources – minerals – topsoil-lumber then sells it back to the new owner?

The housing market is like that land in many ways. It is a basic need and instead of it being used to generate economic benefits for all – neighborhoods – purchases – lifestyle – it is being pillaged to the point where it actually kills the limb from which it sprouts and in essence reaches the root system of the economy and kills it off. Like that land which was purchased, to go forward with life and neighborhoods and the like, it was stripped down to bare and then the new owners were told they had to buy the basic elements – topsoil, etc. back again at a greater cost.

To me it is different because the seller did not create the need. They just capitalized on the transaction. Bigger versions of that capitalization are the scandals involving the home mortgage industry.

Keating 5 and "The Big Short"

Remember the Savings and Loan scandal of the 1980s with the Keating 5 and the recent book/movie "The Big Short?" In both cases home mortgages were at the center. In one case it was a "busting out" of the small Savings and Loans banks across the nation. In the other it was a series of predatory lending.

Here are articles on both.

A BRIEF HISTORY OF - The Keating Five

By Alyssa Fetini Wednesday, Oct. 08, 2008

Following the deregulation of savings and loan associations (S&Ls) in the early 1980's, several of these banks began taking greater liberties with depositors' money, sinking it into risky real estate ventures and junk bonds in an effort to reap maximum profits. Fearful about the future of the vast amounts of feder-ally-insured money being invested, the Federal Home Loan Bank Board (FHLBB) instituted a cap on the amount of money S&L's were allowed to place in such volatile instruments. An investiga-tion into Lincoln Savings and Loan uncovered flagrant violations of these regulations, exceeding the limit by over $615 million.

But before any measures could be taken against the company, five Senators came calling at the FHLBB, requesting that the charges against Lincoln not be pursued, on the basis that the S&L was a major employer in their states. These Senators —John McCain (D-AZ) , John Glenn (D-OH), Alan Cranston (D-CA), Donald Riegle (D-MI) and Dennis DeConcini (D-AZ) — had little in common. Most of them came from different states and different parts of the po-litical spectrum. One of the only elements that linked the men to-gether was Charles Keating. The banker had been a major con-tributor to each of their campaigns, donating close to $1.4 million dollars total. Keating also considered John McCain to be a close personal friend, with whom he'd shared vacations and business ventures.

Their pleas bought Lincoln more time, but the company was ulti-mately seized by the FHLBB two years later. Its bailout cost tax-payers over $3 billion; thousands of Lincoln investors lost their life savings.

The magnitude of Lincoln's collapse and the fraud charges later brought against Keating led the Senate Ethics Committee to launch an investigation into the conduct of the five Senators — now known as the Keating Five — who were thought to have improperly intervened with regulators to protect a campaign contributor.

For more click the link below –

http://content.time.com/time/business/article/0,8599,1848150,00.html

Sound familiar – well it should because it happened again from 2000 to 2008 - this lead to the Great Recession. In the recently released book and subsequent movie "The Big Short" this escapade is explained in detail. Here is an excerpt from a Forbes article clearly outlining the complexity of this fiasco as written by Barry Ritholtz in the Washington Post. Try to keep up with all the moving pieces – just like a game of "Three Card Monty" – who's got the queen, who's got the queen? It is a complex process just like the Quants as they were called which were the algorithms that validated these fake securities. There is an old saying – "If you can't dazzle them with brilliance baffle them with bullshit" – this step by step Rube Goldberg mechanism seems to try and do both at Herculean effort levels.

The story of the 2008 financial crisis

So let's recap the basic facts: why did we have a financial crisis in 2008?

Barry Ritholtz fills us in on the history with an excellent series of articles in the Washington Post:

In 1998, banks got the green light to gamble: The Glass-Steagall legislation, which separated regular banks and investment banks, was repealed in 1998. This allowed banks, whose deposits were guaranteed by the FDIC, i.e. the government, to engage in highly risky business.

Low interest rates fueled an apparent boom: Following the dotcom bust in 2000, the Federal Reserve dropped rates to 1 percent and kept them there for an extended period. This caused a spiral in anything priced in dollars (i.e., oil, gold) or credit (i.e., housing) or liquidity driven (i.e., stocks).

Asset managers sought new ways to make money: Low rates meant asset managers could no longer get decent yields from municipal bonds or Treasurys. Instead, they turned to high-yield mortgage-backed securities.

The credit rating agencies gave their blessing: The credit rating agencies — Moody's, S&P and Fitch had placed an AAA rating on these junk securities, claiming they were as safe as U.S. Treasurys.

Fund managers didn't do their homework: Fund managers relied on the ratings of the credit rating agencies and failed to do adequate due diligence before buying them and did not understand these instruments or the risk involved.

Derivatives were unregulated: Derivatives had become a uniquely unregulated financial instrument. They are exempt from all oversight, counter-party disclosure, exchange listing requirements, state insurance supervision and, most important, reserve requirements. This allowed AIG to write $3 trillion in derivatives while reserving precisely zero dollars against future claims.

The SEC loosened capital requirements: In 2004, the Securities and Exchange Commission changed the leverage rules for just five Wall Street banks. This exemption replaced the 1977 net capitalization rule's 12-to-1 leverage limit. This allowed unlimited leverage for Goldman Sachs [GS], Morgan Stanley, Merrill Lynch (now part of Bank of America [BAC]), Lehman Brothers (now defunct) and Bear Stearns (now part of JPMorganChase–[JPM]). The banks ramped leverage to 20-, 30-, even 40-to-1. Extreme leverage left little room for error. By 2008, only two of the five banks had survived, and those two did so with the help of the bailout.

The federal government overrode anti-predatory state laws. In 2004, the Office of the Comptroller of the Currency federally preempted state laws regulating mortgage credit and national banks, including anti-predatory lending laws on their books (along with lower defaults and foreclosure rates). Following this change, national lenders sold increasingly risky loan products in those states. Shortly after, their default and foreclosure rates increased markedly.

Compensation schemes encouraged gambling: Wall Street's compensation system was—and still is—based on short-term performance, all upside and no downside. This creates incentives to take excessive risks. The bonuses are extraordinarily large and they continue–$135 billion in 2010 for the 25 largest institutions and that is after the meltdown.

Wall Street became "creative": The demand for higher-yielding paper led Wall Street to begin bundling mortgages. The highest yielding were subprime mortgages. This market was dominated by non-bank originators exempt from most regulations.

*Private sector lenders fed the demand: These mortgage origina-
tors' lend-to-sell-to-securitizers models had been holding mortgages for a very short period. This allowed them to relax underwriting standards, abdicating traditional lending metrics such
as income, credit rating, debt-service history and loan-to-value.*

*Financial gadgets milked the market: "Innovative" mortgage
products were developed to reach more subprime borrowers.
These include 2/28 adjustable-rate mortgages, interest-only
loans, piggy-bank mortgages (simultaneous underlying mortgage
and home-equity lines) and the notorious negative amortization
loans (borrower's indebtedness goes up each month). These mortgages defaulted in vastly disproportionate numbers to traditional
30-year fixed mortgages.*

*Commercial banks jumped in: To keep up with these newfangled
originators, traditional banks jumped into the game. Employees
were compensated on the basis of loan volume, not quality.*

*Derivatives exploded uncontrollably: CDOs provided the first "infi-
nite market"; at height of crash, derivatives accounted for 3 times
the global economy.*

*The boom and bust went global. Proponents of the Big Lie ignore
the worldwide nature of the housing boom and bust. A <u>McKinsey
Global Institute</u> report noted "from 2000 through 2007, a remark-
able run-up in global home prices occurred."*

*Fannie and Freddie jumped in the game late to protect their
profits: Nonbank mortgage underwriting exploded from 2001 to
2007, along with the private label securitization market, which
eclipsed Fannie and Freddie during the boom. The vast majority
of subprime mortgages — loans at the heart of the global crisis
— were underwritten by unregulated private firms. These were
lenders who sold the bulk of their mortgages to Wall Street, not
to Fannie or Freddie. Indeed, these firms had no deposits, so they
were not under the jurisdiction of the Federal Deposit Insurance
Corp. or the Office of Thrift Supervision.*

*Fannie Mae and Freddie Mac market share declined. The rela-
tive market share of Fannie Mae and Freddie Mac dropped from
a high of 57 percent of all new mortgage originations in 2003,
down to 37 percent as the bubble was developing in 2005-06.
More than 84 percent of the subprime mortgages in 2006 were*

issued by private lending institutions. The government-sponsored enterprises were concerned with the loss of market share to these private lenders — Fannie and Freddie were chasing profits, not trying to meet low-income lending goals.

It was primarily private lenders who relaxed standards: Private lenders not subject to congressional regulations collapsed lending standards, the GSEs. Conforming mortgages had rules that were less profitable than the newfangled loans. Private securitizers — competitors of Fannie and Freddie — grew from 10 percent of the market in 2002 to nearly 40 percent in 2006. As a percentage of all mortgage-backed securities, private securitization grew from 23 percent in 2003 to 56 percent in 2006.

http://www.forbes.com/sites/stevedenning/2011/11/22/5086/

Who is responsible for such "irresponsibility"? Why are they still walking around free? As a comedian once said, "these guys are walking around and Martha Stewart went to jail" – why?

Recently I heard a great expression about all of this – "They may be too big to fail but they're not too big to jail!"

Starbucks Recession

I called it the Starbucks Recession – why? Because even though times were very tough for some reason, we still seemed to have enough cash for those $4 lattes – it didn't impact the daily economy, this scheme of defrauding the American public just went after the big long-term numbers. As the famous bank robber Willie Sutton said when asked, "Why did you rob those banks?" – He responded, "Cause that's where they keep the money". The S&Ls and the mortgage lenders and the SWAPs were where they kept the money. But in the long run it was bigger than just the money, it was the core of society.

During these two mortgage based recessions we saw the beginning and finally a breakdown of the family system, predicated on a need for a two-income household, no one home to supervise the children, an introduction of the home entertainment system, gaming systems and personal computers. To me, this was the start of the digital economy that was purposely leveraged by the constructed demise of the American Dream and an effort to create an oligarchy of banks and lending machines. See the chart below to get an idea of the final aftermath of all these gyrations.

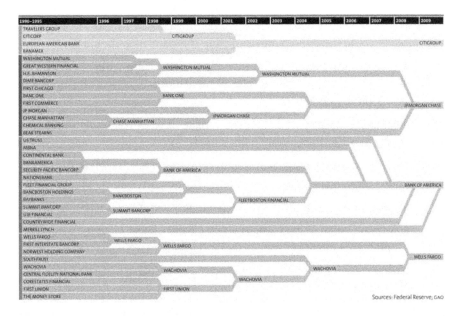

Sources: Federal Reserve; GAO

Building the "Millennials"

The term Millennial refers to the group born after 2000. Gen-i or generation interactive is a term I came up with to combat the simplicity of the term "Millennials." The term "Millennials," to me, just has to do with a date or time and not an actual belief system. "Millennials" are just born at a certain time. It doesn't mean they live the life - it's just a date. Some actually purposely go off the grid , embracing the 1960s commune-like mentality. And "Digital Natives" kind of means the same, but there could be a slightly different birth date. Gen-i means that they are in-it-to-win-it and they can't help it. These young people are at the core of the movement because of both age and lifestyle combined. They're in school now, shaping how we teach by how they learn, and subsequently they'll be consuming and producing by those same patterns. They are the end-user we are designing the society for today.

> In my humble opinion here is the definition of Gen-i. Gen-i stands for generation interactive, isolated, iterative, Internet driven, immaterial, isogonics, isomorphic, (cyber) itinerant, inoculated, etc.

http://patrickaievoli.com/gen-ithe-rise-of-generation-interactive/

But how did they get like this? How did this generation become all of these things and behave as they do? Let's look at some definitions and later statistics as to whether or not this Gen-i is actually all of these things. –

> (Cyber) Itinerant: traveling from place to place: staying in a place for only a short amount of time – "ADD and ADHD"

Immaterial: not important or significant "whatever"

Inoculated: to introduce something into the mind of – "media buzz"

Interactive: designed to respond to the actions, commands, etc., of a user – or: requiring people to talk with each other or do things together — "kind of opposites?"

Ironic: using words that mean the opposite of what you really think especially in order to be funny – "hipsters"

Isogonic: exhibiting equivalent relative growth of parts such that size relations remain constant

Isolated: occurring alone or once – "all day screen time"

Isomorphic: being of identical or similar form, shape, or structure – "nonconforming hipsters"

Iterative: relating to or being iteration of an operation or procedure – endless scrolling and smartphone time

Below I have put together an ironic? rubric to determine what is derived from combinations of each of these components – let's see if I am correct in my assumptions.

Gen-iDentifier	Gamer	Geek	Goth	Hipster
Itinerant	x	x	x	x
Immaterial	x	x		x
Inoculated	x	x	x	x
Interactive	x	x		
Ironic	x	x	x	xxxxx
Isogonic	x		x	
Isolated	x		x	
Isomorphic	x	x	x	xxxxx
Iterative	x		x	xxxxx

If you put all of these pieces together it does seem to represent the tendencies of this age group. They sit around on adult-like play dates staring at their phones. They are in the moment but isolated at the same time, they hop from topic to topic thinking they are multitasking and believe they are interacting - but not really speaking or acknowledging their friends – you know the human ones.

They act in an ironic fashion when they don't even understand fully the principle that they are wishing to be ironic about. Which in itself is amazingly ironic – literally (proper use by the way). They try not to conform as they appear and look exactly like each other in an isomorphic manner. And they scroll and click through iteration after iteration of the same Facebook, Instagram, Tinder, Twitter, etc., page over and over like a medieval French prince (Seinfeld steal).

Chapter 4

Moved elsewhere
Herding them up

The next stage is to move the calf away from the herd to a new location so that the proper rearing can occur, and that usually includes stimulation towards a desired end product.

During this time of a need for double income – again caused by a tremendous rise in base necessities – mortgages – the need for day care in the United States also rose dramatically. Now again as we speak to this metaphor I do want to keep reiterating who the players are in this scenario. All of this is happening through the actions of the "ranchers" at the bequest of the "marketplace" - the ones who truly stand to benefit.

Rise of Day Care

In a previous section we discussed the rise of childcare. And in response to this new dynamic, many families were faced with what has come to be called a non-traditional schedule. During even the "Baby Boom" years there was a parent at home all day especially during the critical years of childhood. Now at the end of the day or even during the day children were "babysat" with technology, from the earliest days of the television to the recent times of the computer.

> *The American Academy of Pediatrics is perhaps the most influential organization to recommend kids between ages three and 18 use screens for a maximum of two hours daily; and kids younger than three should avoid screens altogether, the academy says. But that's not because researchers think digital media is inherently harmful. "If used appropriately, it's wonderful," Marjorie Hogan, a pediatrician at Hennepin County Medical Center in Minneapolis, told NPR. "We don't want to demonize media, because it's going to be a part of everybody's lives increasingly, and we have to teach children how to make good choices around it, how to limit*

it and how to make sure it's not going to take the place of all the other good stuff out there.

... If they're spending five hours in front of the TV, not outside playing, doing homework, or interacting with the parent, that's a problem."

http://www.theatlantic.com/education/archive/2015/01/the-surprising-amount-of-time-kids-spend-looking-at-screens/384737/

"Millennials are spending as many as 18 hours a day skimming the Web, watching TV, texting, playing videogames and using social media, among other activities, according to data from Crowdtrap and Ipsos MediaCT, and arranged by Statista.

Millennials Rack Up 18 Hours of Media Use Per Day

Average time millennials in the U.S. spend interacting with media per day (hh:mm)*

03:34	03:12	02:19	01:47	01:47
Browse the internet	Social networking	Watch live TV	Play video games	Watch timeshifted TV
01:15	01:15	01:04	01:04	00:32
Go to the movies	Listen to the radio	Use email, text, texting apps	Talk about news/ products/brands	Read print magazines /newspapers

* media activities are not mutually exclusive; based on a 2014 survey among 839 U.S. adults aged 18-36

THE WALL STREET JOURNAL.   Source: Crowdtap, Ipsos MediaCT ⓒⓘⓔ **statista**

These aren't counted as consecutive activities, mind you. The days of watching live TV for an hour and then heading over to the desktop to dial up are long gone. Out there is a kid who has the DVR burning through "Scandal," a laptop open to Twitter and a smartphone humming to "Minecraft" at the same time.

That one hour counts as three hours of consumption (however questionable the quality). Take heart, Old Media, some 30 minutes a day are still cordoned off for the printed word."

– Brian R. Fitzgerald

And here is a chart on the rise of sales of computer devices.

Computers, smartphones, and tablet sales: 1975-2011

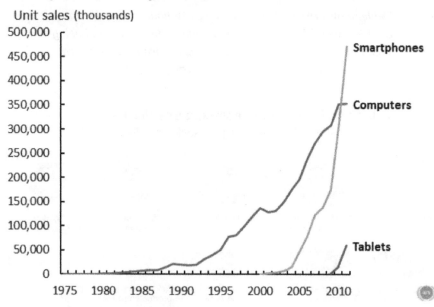

Have you started to notice a correlation between home prices, babies born and computer sales? It all seems to come together to create a "perfect storm." Now the home prices and computer sales go in unison, but the birth rates don't spike in coordination. So what's a girl to do? The question I have been asked a million times is, "how do you make money from the Internet"? Simple answer, just treat it like a shopping center or a mall for one thing. But, companies who profess to "do no harm" are doing much harm, much better by doing - harm. – but they could change that process. "I will drink your milkshake", is a great line, spoken in a movie depicting the early pioneering days of another new economy - oil. So it is understandable when the care of the human falls to a new level of disrespect.

Another version of them being "moved elsewhere" is a mental positioning not necessarily physically moved. In a recent article on LinkedIn I wrote about the social interaction level of this new 12-15 year old demographic. Here it is again to review.

Just say "no"

Is it my imagination (or old age) or does the current generation first answer "no" to every question even if they know the answer and it is almost rhetorical? Whenever I ask a young person, today, almost anything – "is this Main Street?" (while I'm standing under the sign – ok that I do for fun) or "do you know the time"... the first answer is "not sure" or "no I don't."

Seems like the first step is to disengage - to not be civil or to not be social. Ironic in a Brooklyn hipster kind of way – not!

I think I know the reason why?

September 11, 2001 a lot of these current "millennials" were just 9 or 10 years old. They watch as the whole world tumbled and basically everything became immediately suspicious and untrustworthy. Their parents probably felt that way as well and then drilled it into their psyches for protection in a very unsettling world. This was done for pure survival and protection. However it has seemed to undermine the exact strength they need to go forward – some kind of faith and rational belief that the Sun will come up.

Couple this with an economic collapse that ruined many people's retirements and savings and resulted in many firings and job relocations and now you have basically a shell shocked populace. All in all I do think we – people- have held it together very well.

However it seems that it's – "No" to learning, "No" to working through it, "No" to socializing, "No" to just about anything that is long term and not immediate. Why plan long term if there might not be a long term? Why save or trust in anything if it didn't work for your parents.

Over 80% of all families do not have a savings account of any nature over $50,000.00 and that is including 50 year olds! Does working hard really payoff at all anymore? Doesn't seem so – does it? A student answered that they were just going to become a celebrity like KimYe. They were kind of serious – their face said it. Another student put it like this "You had Generation X and Generation Y now you have Generation Y Bother?" You can't blame them.

It's not like they went through World War II or the Great Depression but to them 9/11 and the economic collapse of 2008 felt like it. And in my opinion they were pretty close.

So I understand the "No" but at some point you have to say, "Yes" to something and get on with your life. Many generations have done just that. They moved forward and built their lives. Nobody really gets a trophy for 5th and 6th place in life. In my opinion you need to say "Yes". If not the "No's" will definitely have it and you're pretty much screwed.

https://www.linkedin.com/pulse/
just-say-patrick-aievoli?trk=mp-author-card

Now this may sound dismissive to both the author and the subject, but just the other morning Tom Brokaw was asked why there was so much dissent within the populace and he actually named these two reasons: 9/11 and the 2008 financial collapse. But, why the common thread? Is it that apparent to everyone but we just don't say it out loud?

Maybe it is because years ago we had bigger family groups living in the same town, just blocks from each other. My father bought our house's plot from his mother-in-law and built our house himself after work every night for five years until we moved into it. From the back porch of that house I could see five other immediate relatives' homes. We didn't feel the need to move elsewhere – it was our town. For real - it was our town. I had over fifty immediate relatives at back yard cookouts. So we never felt in danger or scared or anything but comfortable. Large dinners at holiday times were very common. Going over each other's house was very common, happened almost every day. My mother's family ran a local grocery butcher store and everybody in town knew us by first name. At Christmas the store was filled with vats of codfish soaking loosening it up to form what we called in Italian "Baccala"..If anyone would offer it "Baccala" – I would reply "for safety" – in my head not out loud because you would get slapped across the face with some very tough codfish. But pretty much that was our biggest fear at the time.

Now have we purposely tried to keep our children in a separate small space as a means of protecting them from the harm we are seeing all around, a harm we can't be there to protect them from.

This leads to keeping the "calves" in a small place where we can keep an eye on them – you know "buckle them up for safety."

Chapter 5
Kept in a small space
Crating them up

As stated in the previous section childcare has come of age in this new generational family structure. It has become an absolute necessity in many cases. Not a luxury, but a necessity. But, at what cost and what effect has it had? These are not "free range" calves that have the ability to go off on their own and experiment with life. These are "veal" kept in a small space and stimulated just enough and in a specific direction to develop the desired end product.

As "Boomers" growing up we were able to go out to play in the morning and not come home until the lights came on at night. Sure there was trouble from Leopold and Loeb, the Lindbergh Baby, Sacco and Vanzetti. There were always problems and issues with just plain bad things happening. But the fear level wasn't the same. Today, parents are being brought up on charges for simply letting their kid walk home from school or play in a park until sundown.

(CNN)A Maryland family -- the subjects of national headlines when they were accused of neglect for letting their children, ages 6 and 10, walk home alone from a park -- are under investigation again. This time, the children were taken into custody by police officers and held for hours by police and Child Protective Services, according to the family.

"I can't believe we are going through this again," said Danielle Meitiv of Silver Spring, Maryland, in a local television interview. "I can't believe they kept the kids for hours. It's 10:30 at night. They've been missing since six o'clock."

Meitiv and her husband dropped their children off at a park at 4:00 p.m. ET Sunday and told them to return home two hours later. When the kids didn't return by about 6:30 p.m., they started looking for them and grew concerned."

http://www.cnn.com/2015/04/13/living/feat-maryland-free-range-parenting-family-under-investigation-again/

How did all this come about? Were there that many instances of abuse or abductions or was this just a means of spreading fear that would basically paralyze the populace? Why were these parents subjected to such treatment because they allowed their kids to walk home from school or play in the park?

Starting from the 1980s baby slings, car seats, pre-screened play dates, bubble wrapping kids to protect them while maybe putting them in harm's way resulting in way too much screen time?

Seemingly parents were less stressed to have them at home where they could micro-manage and hover like helicopter parents? Electronics gave parents the tools to alleviate guilt; at the same time these tools diminished real participation and learning to work towards actual goals.

The tools parents gave children may have made them prey for "ranchers" to corral easier? We, as parents, positioned them in front of the screen in hopes that it would help them in an arena where we weren't the leaders. But our ignorance of this space allowed them to become overly available for the "feeding frenzy" of content. Just look at the statistics on the increase of screen time for 2013 to 2014.

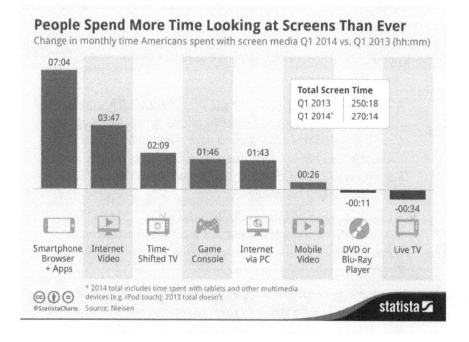

People Spend More Time Looking at Screens Than Ever

Change in monthly time Americans spent with screen media Q1 2014 vs. Q1 2013 (hh:mm)

	Total Screen Time
Q1 2013	250:18
Q1 2014*	270:14

07:04	03:47	02:09	01:46	01:43	00:26	-00:11	-00:34
Smartphone Browser + Apps	Internet Video	Time-Shifted TV	Game Console	Internet via PC	Mobile Video	DVD or Blu-Ray Player	Live TV

* 2014 total includes time spent with tablets and other multimedia devices (e.g. iPod touch); 2013 total doesn't

@StatistaCharts   Source: Nielsen

statista

Game Boys (Girls)

One of the first devices that really broke the blood brain barrier was in my estimation the Nintendo Game Boy. Now you had the distraction in your hand 24/7/365.

In a summary of articles here are some statistics on units sold and usage:

> "As part of the _fourth generation of gaming_, the Game Boy competed with the _Sega Game Gear_, _Atari Lynx_, and the _TurboExpress_. Despite these other handheld consoles,[9] the Game Boy was a tremendous success. The Game Boy and its successor, the _Game Boy Color_,[6] have both, combined, sold 118.69 million units worldwide. Upon its release in the United States, it sold its entire shipment of one million units within a few weeks."
>
> _https://en.wikipedia.org/wiki/Game_Boy#cite_note-10_

Here is a viewpoint on children with ASD, ADD and ADHD and their use of devices like Game Boy.

> _CONCLUSIONS_
>
> _These results suggest that children with ASD and those with ADHD may be at particularly high risk for significant problems related to video game play, including excessive and problematic video game use. Attention problems, in particular, are associated with problematic video game play for children with ASD and ADHD, and role-playing games appear to be related to problematic game use particularly among children with ASD. Although longitudinal research is needed to examine the outcomes of problematic video game use in these special populations, general population studies have shown that problematic game use can have significant detrimental effects. Thus, the current findings indicate a need for heightened awareness and assessment of problematic video game use in clinical care settings for children with ASD and ADHD._
>
> _http://pediatrics.aappublications.org/content/pediatrics/early/2013/07/23/peds.2012-3956.full.pdf_

So in trying to resolve the issues of keeping our kids safe and happy and trying to keep sane ourselves we have possibly led them down the path right into the mouth of demise. Where we think we are giving them something to connect with, we have actually disconnected them from life and into the waiting arms of the "machine" that has turned them into a consumable and consuming life form.

And how long has this been going on? Well just look at the date of this earliest version – 1989 - perfect timing for the first housing jump. By 1989 the first wave of children born to the "housing bubble parents" were around 4 to 5, just about the age when they had to be "entertained" but indoors and not let to run free range through the neighborhood. Voila, here is the perfect solution and training ground - but for what?

> Online games incorporate challenges that compel players to continually hone their skills. As players strive to advance to higher game stages, they can become readily immersed in the action. For some players, immersion can result in their disregarding the outside world.
>
> The psychological arousal that players experience is akin to flow, which can be defined as a state of optimal experience that entails participants becoming totally immersed in the action (Csikszentmihalyi, 1975). Indeed, online games generate considerable pleasure for players, often causing them to lose track of time within the fantastical world of cyber games (Griffiths, Davies, & Chappell, 2004; Rau, Peng, & Yang, 2006). Some players become so immersed in online gaming that it affects them adversely. For example, players have been observed to drop out of school, quit jobs, and distance themselves from friends and family (Griffiths et al., 2004; Young, 2009).

Is this replacing other avenues for serotonin – replacing the love of parent – of friends – of other accomplishments? And does more time away from parent create more of a need for acceptance by device? In essence, is the device and its world replacing the parent?

iPods and iPhones and iPads – oh my!

If you knew anything about Steve Jobs you would know his love of music and especially the Beatles. What seemed to be his "dream project" once he returned to Apple was the iPod. He would speak of it as a revolutionary – insanely great idea! But take a step back for a moment and realize that Jobs always had a multi-level plan going on.

Anyone of our – 1955 and on - generation remembered the transistor radio with the earplug. Well Jobs basically just updated that to a new device called the iPod. He would say "ten thousand songs that fit into your jean pocket." Yep, but we had that back in the 1960s – a simple 9 volt transistor radio. Here is that radio and an iPod pictured side by side.

What's the difference? One provided Jobs with a cash machine into your pocket and the other was a one-time purchase (except for the batteries). It was a huge move – insanely great but not without cost. Have you ever looked at your iTunes purchases for a year? Now those are insanely great – for Steve but not so much for your family budget.

It also introduced the touch screen capabilities for the first time in a simple way at first that soon led to the actual touch screen?

Here is the first version of Apple's move into that space - the Apple Newton. Notice the similarities to the iPhone – this was just a prototype for that new cash machine we have all come to love and not be able to do without.

The Apple App Store revenues for 2015 are record breaking (see article excerpt below). Apple's App Store Saw $1.7B in Billings and Broke Customer Records In July

Perhaps to counter concerns over iPhone sales and China, Apple this week released numbers related to the App Store's growth that demonstrate the very real impact China is having on its app ecosystem and developer community.

The company said that, in July, it had its largest number of transacting customers with over $1.7 billion in billings. In addition, the same month broke records for China, too, which also saw the largest number of transacting customers, Apple said.

To date, the company has paid out $33 billion to App Store developers, it said – $8 billion of which was in 2015 alone. For comparison's sake, just over a year ago, Apple said it had paid $20 billion to developers.

http://techcrunch.com/2015/08/07/apples-app-store-saw-1-7b-in-billings-and-broke-customer-records-in-july/

Now let's introduce the main attraction – the main event – the true dream machine – the cash making – credit card emptying mother of them all - the iPad.

In-game purchases

Today gaming is fast becoming an addiction. People are playing Candy Crush – Angry Birds whatever they can, to be distracted from everyday stress. That's a good thing, again to a degree. But these seemingly innocuous games are actually mining user data to determine whereabouts, patterns, hours of use, etc.

And what happens to these kids playing these games not to count the time wasted but the push to purchase items in the game.

Here are some examples – we've all heard the stories.

This Kid Blew $2,500 on In-Game Purchases in Just 10 Minutes

Shameless in-game purchases aimed at kids have been in the news recently. But this five-year-old kid spent more than most: he blew $2,500 on in-game junk in just 10 minutes. That's impressive.

The boy in question is Danny Kitchen. The game is Zombie v Ninja, which is "free" for download on iTunes. When he was playing on his folks' iPad one day, he asked for the iTunes password so he could download game. Danny's parents typed it in, saying they were reassured by the fact that the game was listed as being free, and left him to get on with playing the thing.

Danny then went in-app purchase crazy, buying stacks of the $100 in-game keys and weapon packs, and racking up an enormous credit card bill for his mom. "I was worried and I felt sad," said Danny, when he found out, adding: "I'm banned from the iPad now." Too right.

http://gizmodo.com/5987799/
this-kid-blew-2500-on-in-game-purchases-in-just-10-minutes

Now, let's look, even further at the peer-pressure exerted on these kids by celebrity in-game purchasing.

Kim Kardashian's Hollywood

Kim Kardashian's kids game has been criticized for its in-app purchases

Kanye West went on Twitter yesterday to rant against smart-phone apps that allow kids to make in-game purchases. "F–k any game company that puts in-app purchases on kids games!!!" wrote Kanye on Twitter.

But he forgot one important thing: his wife, Kim Kardashian, has her own game that allows its own in-app purchases. "Kim

Kardashian: Hollywood" offers a bevy of in-app purchases for up to $40.

Last year, Ayelet Waldman, the bestselling author of Bad Mother and wife of novelist Michael Chabon, _complained_ on Twitter that Kardashian's app "tricked" her 11-year-old son into spending $120 on Kardashian's in-app store.

Kim _defended_ the game's app-purchase feature in a television interview, telling Today's Matt Lauer, "I think you just have to be responsible, and don't have your credit card linked to where your kid can just spend if they want to, or ask permission."

It's advice Kanye may want to take.

http://time.com/4069228/
kanye-west-kim-kardashian-in-app-purchases-games/

This is even happening in other countries as well, so it is not an American issue alone.

Seven-Year-Old Jurassic World Fan Spends £4,000 of His Father's Money on In-Game Transactions

Mobile gaming might not be put at the same level of seriousness as other platforms but for a 32 year old father from Crawley, UK it couldn't get any more serious business. This is so because his seven-year-old son was able to charge his credit card with £4,000 by making in-game transactions on Jurassic World, an iPad game.

Mohamed Shugaa, the 32 year old father, says that he knew his son had seen his Apple ID password but he had no clue his son had memorized it. The kid, Faisal Shugaa, was able to use that password to make as many as 65 transactions upgrading the dinosaurs and so on.

His son was into the Jurassic World game so much that at one point he spent £1,500 in one hour! You can expect how shocked and furious the father was.

http://segmentnext.com/2015/12/31/7-year-old-jurassic-
world-fan-spends-4000-of-his-fathers-money-on-in-game-
transactions/

What is causing these kids to basically pilfer their parents' money and just spend away? Not because it is easy, I suggest, but because they want to belong to the herd.

And what is that herd worth? We all hear about these numbers – these valuations of companies – FaceBook valued at $15 Billion – Twitter valued at $5 Billion – What's App purchased for $19 Billion – with only 19 employees.

In the next section we will breakdown exactly how much this is worth financially but for now let's focus on what it is worth to your kids.

What happens when you don't fit into Kim's Hollywood Squad or you're not allowed in the right group on Facebook?

Cyber Bullying

According to Webster here is the definition of

Cyberbullying

1:   the electronic posting of mean-spirited messages about a person (as a student) often done anonymously

We have all heard of it and have even read about the effects of this relatively new form of classic abuse, but now it follows you 24/7/365. Now it is responsible for probably more deaths globally than its analogue predecessor ever was. The stories are in the news and unfortunately for many they are even more close at hand.

Social Media Cyber Bullying Linked to Teen Depression

Social media use is hugely common among teenagers, said Michele Hamm, a researcher in pediatrics at the University of Alberta, but the health effects of cyberbullying on social media sites is largely unknown. Regular, face-to-face bullying during the teen years may double the risk of depression in adulthood, and bullying's effects can be as bad, or worse than, child abuse, studies show.

A depressing effect

In the new review, Hamm and her colleagues combed through studies on cyberbullying and social media, finding 36 that investigated the effects of cyberbullying on health in teens ages 12 to 18. Although the studies examined different health outcomes and sometimes defined cyberbullying differently, one finding stood out.

"There were consistent associations between exposure to cyberbullying and increased likelihood of depression," Hamm told Live Science. [8 Tips for Parents of Teens with Depression]

The studies covered a variety of social sites, but Facebook was the most common—between 89 percent and 97.5 percent of the teens who used social media had a Facebook account. Seventeen of the 36 studies analyzed looked at how common cyberbullying was, and the researchers found that a median of 23 percent of teens reported being targeted. About 15 percent reported bullying someone online themselves.

Two studies examined the prevalence of so-called "bully-victims," meaning teens who both bully others and are bullied. Research on offline bullying shows these kids to be most at-risk for mental health problems. One study found that 5.4 percent of teens were bully-victims, while the other reported a prevalence of 11.2 percent.

http://www.scientificamerican.com/article/ social-media-cyber-bullying-linked-to-teen-depression/

This is just one account of this growing problem. There have been bullies since Cain killed Abel but now the consistent, invisible and omnipotent qualities of this act has resonated its strength.

Today it goes even further to - in my humble opinion - psychotic behavior.

Catfishing

Known for what it is today this appears to be one of the more insane uses of the Internet and a little horror movie-esque. Here is the current definition of "Catfishing".

Catfishing

a person who sets up a false personal profile on a social networking site for fraudulent or deceptive purposes

We have all heard about it and maybe have even seen the movie from 2011 but it gets even weirder once you start looking into the actual cases.

How to Avoid Becoming a Victim of a 'Catfish'

Notre Dame star linebacker Manti Te'o claims to have been the victim of an elaborate online hoax. MTV's Catfish is a show about a similar online romance, one which also raises doubts about its authenticity.

Online impersonation with the intent of engaging in a relationship is becoming more common. Similar to identity theft, which is when someone steals personal identifiable information from a victim and uses that information in the commission of a crime (fraud, etc.) -- Catfishing is when someone "assumes" a real person's identity and/ or creates a new online persona to engage in an online relationship.

Phishing, which is related to Catfishing, is a common tactic used by online criminals to lure unsuspecting victims to do something which may lead to identity theft or other nefarious activities.

The reality is that this could happen to anyone that uses the Internet. Your own online persona could be used as a "catfish" profile or you might be duped into believing someone isn't who they purport to be.

http://www.huffingtonpost.com/jonathan-rajewski/how-to-avoid-becoming-a-v_1_b_2507220.html

This is the perfect example of taking something meant to be benevolent and destroying it to the point where it actually does damage to people who may have stumbed into a deceptive practice as innocent bystanders on the Information Super Highway. We might question whether anyone can still afford to say they are just an innocent bystander.

Opportunists or entrepreneurs - who was behind this?

If you are asking was there a plan to all this, in my opinion the answer is that this was all premeditated. Build a device that keeps going in and out of your pocketbook - a device that enables the practice of all forms of pressure to push these young people and the economy along.

From 1980 to present day, society has witnessed the rise of the personal computer in the home. In a recent documentary on CNN titled "Steve Jobs | Man in the Machine", Jobs is portrayed for what he was: a genius and the mastermind behind the personal computer. In the documentary, Jobs is shown many times using the phrase – "seduced" in reference to using a personal computer. His eyes sparkle when he talks about this and you can almost feel his glee and hubris.

Full disclosure here – I am a huge fan of Jobs – I actually started an outline for a book years before his death called "American Icon" a slight pun on how applications are displayed as icons on a desktop. While his genius is undisputed it may not be for the actual engineering of the physical computer but more so for engineering its need and acceptance by society. His famous phrase of "showing them the need for something they didn't think they needed," just through the pure capability of the machine and its software.

Mr. Jobs was the paramount showman, but we can never know how much was showmanship and how much was he preying on the desire for these users' own hubris. Many early computer wizards thought they were going to be the next Jobs or Wozniak or Gates but the odds of these geeks becoming as omnipotent as Jobs are very low.

I have been involved in this space since the days when the team at Apple started. At McGraw-Hill I was fortunate enough to be given the first Macintosh computer in my division. I got to see this device from almost day one and certainly got to work with some of the software that would make this machine truly a centerpiece in the early stages of this digital revolution.

From the very first days of MacDraw and MacPaint up to the first incarnations of Photoshop, Illustrator and the like, I could see the impact this would have on the media industry. Jobs knew it as well with the minor training in calligraphy he fought for the use of quality typography and a true aesthetic. This was part of the seduction, a temptress using beauty to lure the masses. We felt tremendously empowered when we were part of it at the time – a select few who could do this. We even glorified and demonized them in popular culture.

Video games became a strong target of blame - as they should – sorry but if you get points for killing prostitutes and stealing cars – you also get the blame. In Second Life you could be anyone you wanted to be. The biggest geek could be the biggest hero – an amazing seduction if there ever was one.

But the unusual point for Apple is the development of eWorld – the early Apple developed online village presence. Years before AOL and Netscape started exploring this new space, Apple was building a major online community of learning and sharing. Here is an excerpt form a 2014 article on the twentieth anniversary of eWorld.

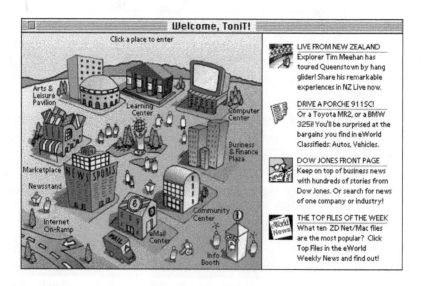

eWorld's main screen.

Remembering eWorld, Apple's forgotten online service

Benj Edwards - Macworld - Jun 9, 2014 3:44 AM

Just before the Internet's meteoric rise in the public conscious-ness, large centralized dial-up services like America Online, Prod-igy, and CompuServe dominated the online landscape.

In this competitive climate 20 years ago, Apple introduced eWorld, a subscription-based information service available to Mac and Newton users. Despite its closure in 1996, eWorld re-mains notable for its city-based interface metaphor and as a sym-bol of Apple's overreach in the era.

Users accessed eWorld through custom client software written by Apple and connected using a traditional dial-up modem hooked to a telephone line. Upon connecting to the service, the eWorld software displayed a playfully-illustrated aerial view of a small city. Each building in the city represented a different topical focus for the service, containing articles, chat rooms, discussion boards, and file downloads centered around various themes.

http://www.macworld.com/article/2202091/remembering-eworld-apples-forgotten-online-service.html

So, not only did Apple see the need for local hardware and software uses, but they went far beyond and attempted a way-too-early move to the Internet - very smart but maybe too smart and too aggressive. They could always iden-tify a "killer app."

Defining a "killer app"

What is a "killer app"? Simply put it is the application that makes any de-vice worth its price - desktop publishing for the Macintosh, business soft-ware for IBM and Windows and on. Here is a quick definition from PCMag Encyclopedia.

killer app

A software application that is exceptionally useful or exciting. Killer apps are innovative and often represent the first of a new breed, and they are extremely successful. For example, in the late 1970's, the VisiCalc spreadsheet was the killer app for the Ap-ple II, providing reason enough to purchase the hardware. Visi-Calc was followed by Lotus 1-2-3 and Excel for the IBM PC. In the early 1990s, the Mosaic Web browser was the killer app for the

Internet. It was quickly followed by Netscape and others. Contrast with filler app and app killer.

http://www.pcmag.com/encyclopedia/term/45817/killer-app

The link between a "killer app" and the Gen-i kids were the killer app for the new economy. Yes, that's right, the actual children not the hardware or the software. Everything was built – hardware and software wise and even "the products were all put on shelves with care – in hopes that soon our friend PayPal would be there." We tried to put this machine into motion before but to no avail – remember the "dot com" bubble bursting in 1999-2000? I sure do because I was right there building a startup. Why did it burst? My opinion is that it got too big too fast and the existing economic powers saw that it was going to be very disruptive, so they simply had it quashed, stopped-dead in its tracks. The "bubble" burst because it was going too fast and could not be steered into the mainstream pockets. Now, as you see it is there, in the traditional brick and mortar corporations.

This 2010 article showed some numerical insight into this current generation's take over of the economy in as far as driving the new economic delivery and behavioral platforms.

DECEMBER 16, 2010

GENERATIONS 2010

Online Activities

BY KATHRYN ZICKUHR

Activities most popular with teens and/or Millennials

Younger Internet users ages 12-33 remain the most active participants in the web's social services. Seventy-three percent of teens and 83% of Millennials use social network sites, significantly more than older generations, especially adults over 55: While half of Younger Boomers use social network sites, only 16% of adults 74 and older have done so. Internet users under 30 are also significantly more likely to communicate via instant message, with roughly two-thirds of teens and Millennials sending and receiving instant messages. Internet users under age 34 are also significantly more likely to read blogs—49% of teens and 43% of Millennials do this.

Teens, meanwhile, are by far the most likely to play online games: 78% play games online, the most popular activity for that age group. Teens are also the most likely group to visit a virtual world such as Second Life—8% of online teens, compared with 4% of internet users 18 and older.

Internet users ages 34-64 have lost their lead over Millennials in certain activities, such as buying products or banking online, as well as in searching for health or religious information. Other areas, such as blogging, were once the domain of teens and Millennials, but are now relatively common throughout most age groups.

http://www.pewinternet.org/2010/12/16/online-activities/

I want to keep reiterating throughout this book that I have made my living and continue to make it doing and teaching interaction design – the method of creating interfaces that are engaging and solve client problems. You know basically the devil incarnate. But it doesn't have to be that way. My super powers can be used for good as well as evil. It is up to you to decide. If my skill set allows a child to blog about her passion for horses then good. If it requires you 4 year old to have your PIN – again not good. If it gives you too much free time away from your lovely children probably not good.

In the next sections we are going to talk about how being kept in a small space leads to being stimulated to just the right amount and in just the right way to generate the desired end result. And once they have been stimulated and they respond correctly how they are corralled into social networks – "herds" – to be sold off in pieces for individual price points. Basically like any commodity but in this metaphor – "veal".

Is this the new economy? Remember the "TechCrunch" blurb –

"In 2015 Uber, the world's largest taxi-company owns no vehicles, Facebook the world's most popular media owner creates no content, Alibaba, the most valuable retailer has no inventory and Airbnb the world's largest accommodation provider owns no real estate."

When was the last time an economic shift of this magnitude occurred? Not just a new means to a new economy but a complete shift in manufacturing to service?

Remember Napster by Sean Parker the music file sharing network? Well that basically destroyed the music industry and it has really never recovered – yet.

Chapter 6
Stimulated just enough
Creating the right mixture

So far we have taken this metaphor from birth to separation to moving the "herd" to gathering them in a small space now to "stimulating them just enough" to produce the end product.

What is that product? Time – time on a screen, time swiping and clicking and using and chatting and "snap chatting" and whatever. Eyeballs and actions equal revenue in this game. And everyone is fighting for that attention.

As you have seen throughout this last chapter, screen time has increased dramatically in the last 5 years. Where is that value for the companies and corporations that advertise and fight for that screen time? Well first we need to validate and explain what we are talking about here.

Online advertising is one of the biggest areas of revenue in this market space. Here are some terms to explain that return on investment.

CPA (Cost-per-Action)

Cost of advertising based on a visitor taking some specifically defined action in response to an ad. Examples of "Actions" include such things as completing a sales transaction, or filling out a form.

CPC *CPC is the abbreviated term for both Cost-per-Click and Cost-per-Customer. Please click on the term you are looking for.*

CPC (Cost-per-Click)

CPC or cost-per-click is the cost of advertising based on the number of clicks received.

CPC (Cost-per-Customer)

CPC or Cost-per-customer is the cost an advertiser pays to acquire a customer.

CPL (Cost-per-lead)

Cost of advertising based on the number of database files (leads) received.

CPM (Cost-per-thousand)

Media term describing the cost of 1,000 impressions. For example, a Web site that charges $1,500 per ad and reports 100,000 impressions has a CPM of $15 ($1,500 divided by 100).

CPO (Cost-per-Order)

Cost of advertising based on the number of orders received. Also called Cost-per-Transaction.

CPS (Cost-per-Sale)

The advertiser's cost to generate one sales transaction. If this is being used in conjunction with a media buy, a cookie can be offered on the content site and read on the advertiser's site after the successful completion of an online sale.

CPT (Cost-per-Transaction) - See CPO (Cost-per-Order)

CPTM (Cost per Targeted Thousand Impressions)

Implying that the audience one is trying to reach is defined by particular demographics or other specific characteristics, such as male golfers age 18-25. The difference between CPM and CPTM is that CPM is for gross impressions, while CPTM is for targeted impressions.

http://www.iab.net/wiki/print/

I know all those terms seem confusing to digest but realize that this is just how valuable your time on the Internet is to these companies. It is truly an entire economy not just fun in the sun time. It has become the biggest industry globally. As David Byrne said, "This ain't no disco – no CBGBs – this ain't no messing around..." They are serious and this is serious. How this happened was a confluence of events best explained by Thomas Freidman.

Someone I truly respect is Thomas Freidman Pulitzer prize-winning author and columnist for the *New York Times*. I advocate his books to my students and to my friends.

In one of his most famous books *The World is Flat* (2004) he listed some of the main contributors towards this "Flattened World," some of which I think are directly related to what we are seeing in our children and our society today.

All of these came together to create the opportunity to use all of those terms you read just previously. If these events did not happen, maybe those tools could not have been so useful to create this new economy?

Here is his list compiled from an article on Wikipedia, but they are the ones from his book.

Friedman Ten "Flatteners":

#1: Collapse of the Berlin Wall – 11/9/89: Friedman called the flattener, "When the walls came down, and the windows came up." The event not only symbolized the end of the Cold War, it allowed people from the other side of the wall to join the economic mainstream. "11/9/89" is a discussion about the Berlin Wall coming down, the "fall" of communism, and the impact that Windows powered PCs (personal computers) had on the ability of individuals to create their own content and connect to one another. At that point, the basic platform for the revolution to follow was created: IBM PC, Windows, a standardized graphical interface for word processing, dial-up modems, a standardized tool for communication, and a global phone network.

#2: Netscape – 8/9/95: Netscape went public at the price of $28. Netscape and the Web broadened the audience for the Internet from its roots as a communications medium used primarily by "early adopters and geeks" to something that made the Internet accessible to everyone from five-year-olds to ninety-five-year-olds. The digitization that took place meant that everyday occurrences such as words, files, films, music, and pictures could be accessed and manipulated on a computer screen by all people across the world.

#3: Workflow software: Friedman's catch-all for the standards and technologies that allowed work to flow. The ability of machines to talk to other machines with no humans involved, as stated by Friedman. Friedman believes these first three forces have become a "crude foundation of a whole new global platform for collaboration." There was an emergence of software protocols

(SMTP – simple mail transfer protocol; HTML – the language that enabled anyone to design and publish documents that could be transmitted to and read on any computer anywhere) Standards on Standards. This is what Friedman called the "Genesis moment of the flat world." The net result "is that people can work with other people on more stuff than ever before." This created a global platform for multiple forms of collaboration. The next six flatteners sprung from this platform.

#4: Uploading: Communities uploading and collaborating on online projects. Examples include open source software, blogs, and Wikipedia. Friedman considers the phenomenon "the most disruptive force of all."

#5: Outsourcing: Friedman argues that outsourcing has allowed companies to split service and manufacturing activities into components which can be subcontracted and performed in the most efficient, cost-effective way. This process became easier with the mass distribution of fiber optic cables during the introduction of the World Wide Web.

#6: Offshoring: The internal relocation of a company's manufacturing or other processes to a foreign land to take advantage of less costly operations there. China's entrance in the WTO (World Trade Organization) allowed for greater competition in the playing field. Now countries such as Malaysia, Mexico, Brazil must compete against China and each other to have businesses offshore to them.

#7: Supply-chaining: Friedman compares the modern retail supply chain to a river, and points to Wal-Mart as the best example of a company using technology to streamline item sales, distribution, and shipping.

#8: Insourcing: Friedman uses UPS as a prime example for insourcing, in which the company's employees perform services – beyond shipping – for another company. For example, UPS repairs Toshiba computers on behalf of Toshiba. The work is done at the UPS hub, by UPS employees.

#9: Informing: Google and other search engines and Wikipedia are the prime example. "Never before in the history of the planet have so many people – on their own – had the ability to find so much information about so many things and about so many other people," writes Friedman. The growth of search engines is tremendous; for example, Friedman states that Google is "now processing

roughly one billion searches per day, up from 150 million just three years ago."

#10: "The Steroids": Wireless, Voice over Internet, and file sharing. Personal digital devices like mobile phones, iPods, personal digital assistants, instant messaging, and voice over Internet Protocol (VoIP). Digital, Mobile, Personal and Virtual – all analog content and processes (from entertainment to photography to word processing) can be digitized and therefore shaped, manipulated and transmitted; virtual – these processes can be done at high speed with total ease; mobile – can be done anywhere, anytime by anyone; and personal – can be done by you.

https://en.wikipedia.org/wiki/The_World_Is_Flat

Please get this book and start here to truly familiarize yourself with what he and many others are saying has happened and what I believe was part of the groundwork that started this huge change in our society. Would the process for "stimulating just enough" have been possible if not for these events?

The planned progression from Newton to iPad to Mobile –

It is important to consider whether this is a natural progression to the touch-screen or part of a plan or something that was seen and capitalized on. Read Friedman's Ten "Flatteners" again – and see if they would be either happening at all or if they would have the potential to do anything without the perfect delivery method and tool.

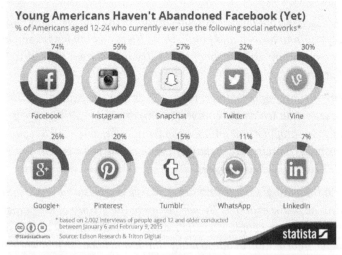

https://d28wbuch0jlv7v.cloudfront.net/images/infografik/normal/chartoftheday_3276_Social_networks_used_by_young_Americans_n.jpg

Another consideration is whether this is just a passing fad of some nature or has now been entrenched into our collective psyche. One hopes the kids just move on from this like Pokemon and Power Rangers, and wonder whether it has had a lasting effect on them.

What's the damage here?

Health issues - nurture and nature – sugar and screen time – brain patterns – did the "ranchers" put together the perfect feed mixer for this generation? Remember veal are put on a specific diet to generate just the right results, usually a heavy milk or cream.

Let's take a look at some research on the increase of screen time – whether computers or television alone with High Fructose Corn Syrup and the advent of ADD/BPD and many other physiological and psychological effects.

Does Too Much Screen Time Make Kids Sick?

Screen time may make your child (chronically) ill.

Posted Apr 03, 2014

Technology is playing a different, and bigger, role in all of our lives, including children's, but that does not make the AAP's recommendation outdated or irrelevant. In fact, the increasing role of technology in our lives should be all the more reason to pay close attention to recommendations like the AAP's that suggested limited screen time for children (and probably for adults too!).

So...Next time you are tempted to let your child watch an extra hour of TV or play that videogame a little longer, you might want to reconsider and send them outside instead. Your decision could have an impact on your child's habits and their overall physical health. If children consistently exceed the recommended two hour limit on screen time, they will be at increased risk for chronic illness in the future! Furthermore, an increase in physical activity is not enough to reverse these effects. Screen time impacts physical health independent of physical activity, so the best solution is simply to reduce screen time, and maybe go to the library and do paper book reading.

References

American Academy of Pediatrics Committee on Public Education. (2001). Children, Adolescents, and Television. Pediatrics, 107(2), 223-6.

Personally, I agree with this so far. Physical activity is a necessity for development obviously, but the question is the balance of that time and whether an imbalance results in conditions like ADHD and the sorts.

Fixated by Screens, but Seemingly Nothing Else

But then she brightened. "But he can't have attention deficit, I know that."

Why? Her son could sit for hours concentrating on video games, it turned out, so she was certain there was nothing wrong with his attention span.

It's an assertion I've heard many times when a child has attention problems. Sometimes parents make the same point about television: My child can sit and watch for hours — he can't have A.D.H.D.

In fact, a child's ability to stay focused on a screen, though not anywhere else, is actually characteristic of attention deficit hyperactivity disorder. There are complex behavioral and neurological connections linking screens and attention, and many experts believe that these children do spend more time playing video games and watching television than their peers.

But is a child's fascination with the screen a cause or an effect of attention problems — or both? It's a complicated question that researchers are still struggling to tease out.

The kind of concentration that children bring to video games and television is not the kind they need to thrive in school or elsewhere in real life, according to Dr. Christopher Lucas, associate professor of child psychiatry at New York University School of Medicine. "It's not sustained attention in the absence of rewards," he said. "It's sustained attention with frequent intermittent rewards."

Does TV affect children's brain development?

With television programs—and even a cable channel—designed and marketed specifically for babies, whether kids under two years of age should be watching becomes an important question. While we are learning more all the time about early brain development, we do not yet have a clear idea how television may affect it. Some studies link early TV viewing with later attention problems, such as ADHD. However, other experts disagree with these results. One study found that TV viewing before age three slightly hurt several measures of later cognitive development, but that between ages three and five it slightly helped reading scores [11]. –

http://www.med.umich.edu/yourchild/topics/tv.htm

Again the term "flow" comes into discussion. Here is an excerpt from a report dealing with online game addiction entitled:

Advanced or Addicted? Exploring the Relationship of Recreation Specialization to Flow Experiences and Online Game Addiction

TSUNG-CHIUNG (EMILY) WU
Department of Tourism, Recreation and Leisure Studies
National Dong Hwa University
Hualien, Taiwan, ROC

DAVID SCOTT
Department of Recreation, Park and Tourism Sciences
Texas A&M University
College Station, TX, USA

CHUN-CHIEH YANG
Institute of Public Affairs Management
National Sun Yat-sen University

Although flow is considered by many to be a positive outcome of participation in leisure activities, some players become so absorbed they manifest addictive tendencies. The meaning of game addiction is contested—the term is colloquially used to describe extreme devotion or state of being absorbed in a game (Holt & Kleiber, 2009). Extreme devotion, however, can lead to single-mindedness such that participation has a negative impact on the individual and his or her loved ones (Partington, Partington, & Olivier, 2009).

The overuse or daily standard use of social media networks to me has to do with the "herd" mentality, especially how it connects to social media networks, peer-pressure and acceptance.

Does Social Network Site Use Affect Student Grades and Learning?

Research on social networking sites and learning achievement is particularly slight when compared to studies of privacy, safety, social capital, and psychological well-being. To date, two studies exemplify the debate surrounding SNS, youth, and educational achievement. A conference paper by Karpinski (2009) received much media attention with findings that college Facebook users have lower GPAs than students who are not users of the site. Karpinski offers several hypotheses for these findings. For example, perhaps Facebook users spend too much time online and less time studying. However, the study did not rigorously examine counter hypotheses and remains a rather exploratory, basic attempt to understand the effect of SNS on learning.

http://onlinelibrary.wiley.com/store/10.1002/asi.21540/asset/21540_ftp

With those questions buzzing around our brain, the next step is to consider whether there has been a long sustainable change going on in our children's patterns, health, socialization, overall patterns since this specific amalgam of nature and nurture took this turn.

Rise of ODD, ADD/Bipolar disorder – oh look...

In full disclosure here, I have never been diagnosed with ADD or Bipolar but such terms were unkown close to 60 years ago. I know now from reading up on the subject that I definitely am both. My mom used to call me "moody," "schizo" and other terms of that time, never derogatory just fearful of not knowing what to do for me. If it wasn't for her I don't know where I would be today. It was her patience and simply her pure love that got me over it. She would sit up with me for hours and days getting me through what I now see as manic episodes. She would be exhausted but she never quit on me. Very few parents have that luxury of time today, which was afforded by my father who never knew the concept of not working – even until his last days. They were an amazing team – I used to say "he pedaled and she steered."

Controversies concerning the diagnosis and treatment of bipolar disorder in children

Erik Parens and Josephine Johnston

In September 2007, a group of researchers made headlines when they reported a forty-fold increase in the number of office visits in which children had a diagnosis of bipolar disorder (BP)[1].

The researchers estimated that whereas, in 1994-1995, in about 25 out of every 100,000 visits a child had a bipolar diagnosis, the number increased to 1,003 per 100,000 by 2002-2003. During the same ten-year period, office visits by adults with a BP diagnosis almost doubled from 905 to 1,679 per 100,000 annually, suggesting that BP diagnoses reported by community-based clinicians have increased across the age span. But the very low base rate of this diagnosis in youth coupled with a rapid rise signaled a major practice change.

Once thought rare in pre-adolescents, BP is now increasingly diagnosed in children, including preschoolers [2]. The drugs used to treat it include mood stabilizers and antipsychotics [3], which carry the risk of significant side effects. Perhaps even more than the diagnosis and treatment of Attention-Deficit/Hyperactivity Disorder (ADHD) and childhood depression before it, the ascension of the BP diagnosis in children and its treatment with medications whose risk/benefit profiles are inadequately established have generated debate in both lay and professional communities.

http://www.ncbi.nlm.nih.gov/pmc/articles/PMC2846895/

Frightening stuff isn't it? The goal here is not to get you running around the house trashing all of the computers, laptops and smart phones. The goal has been to realize that "the kids may not be all right" after all. And also that there are forces busy working on them while you're being busy working for them.

"Vaxxed" and Tribeca Film Festival 2016

Recently actor Robert DeNiro held a press conference to say the film "Vaxxed" was going to be dropped from the line up of the festival. According to the *New York Times,*

In a statement, Robert De Niro, a founder of the festival, wrote: "My intent in screening this film was to provide an opportunity for conversation around an issue that is deeply personal to me and my family. But after reviewing it over the past few days with the Tribeca Film Festival team and others from the scientific community, we do not believe it contributes to or furthers the discussion I had hoped for."

http://www.nytimes.com/2016/03/27/movies/robert-de-niro-pulls-anti-vaccine-documentary-from-tribeca-film-festival.html?_r=0

But later in a *Today* show interview chronicled in an article by the telegraph.com's website, Mr. DeNiro seemed to show a different side.

> *Robert De Niro has waded into the controversy over whether vaccines can cause autism, saying that he believes there is a link and that some children should not be vaccinated.*
>
> *De Niro revealed last month that his 18-year-old son Elliot has autism, and said on Wednesday that he believes certain children are at risk of being harmed by vaccines.*
>
> *The Godfather star is the latest celebrity to make such claims, which have been almost universally rejected by doctors but are accepted by a growing number of parents.*
>
> *"There are a lot of things that are not said," he said on NBC's Today Show. "I as a parent of a child who has autism am concerned, and I want to know the truth."*
>
> *De Niro, 72, made the comments after a film tying the measles, mumps and rubella (MMR) vaccine to autism was pulled from New York's Tribeca film festival, which he co-founded.*
>
> *The film, titled Vaxxed, sparked tremendous backlash for its anti-vaccine position, but the actor said everyone should see it because "there's definitely something to it".*
>
> *He said on Wednesday that there is a "hysteria, a knee-jerk reaction" to dismiss concerns about vaccines, but that he has become convinced that there is a correlation of some sort.*
>
> *"I'm not a scientist but I know because I've seen so much reaction-let's just find out the truth," he said.*
>
> *The Oscar winner said his wife believed Elliot had changed overnight after having a vaccine, and that numerous other parents felt guilt over the fact that vaccines may have harmed their children.*
>
> *http://www.telegraph.co.uk/news/2016/04/13/robert-de-niro-there-is-a-link-between-vaccines-and-autism/*

Here is another recent book and article substantiating beliefs of the manipulations of the findings on the efficiency and culpability of these vaccines.

> *Book Review: 'Master Manipulator' Accuses CDC of Manipulating Science on Autism*
>
> *'Master Manipulator: The Explosive True Story of Fraud, Embezzlement, and Government Betrayal at the CDC' by James Ottar*

Grundvig, with introduction Robert F. Kennedy, Jr. (New York: Sky-horse Publishing). $24.99.

"Grundvig notes that the CDC officials who are alleged in the controversial documentary "Vaxxed" (pulled by the Tribeca Film Festival after pressure from unknown members of the scientific community) to have committed research fraud were the same scientists who brought in Thorsen.

Grundvig highlights the CDC's role as sponsors of hiring the rogue Danish scientist in Chapter 8, "2001: A Data Odyssey," by capturing the May 30, 2001, email exchange between CDC's Dr. Marshalyn Yeargin-Allsopp to José Cordero. She wrote:

"As we discussed on Friday, we have become aware through Poul Thorsen of an exciting opportunity to study the role of MMR vaccine and autism using several registries/existing studies and the repository of biologic specimens and laboratory capabilities in Denmark."

There were two principal legal theories being tested before Special Masters presiding over the Omnibus Autism Proceedings in the NVICP: whether the MMR vaccine caused autism and whether Thimerosal (the mercury-based vaccine preservative) caused autism as well.

Thanks to Thorsen, the CDC had what it needed to help the secretary of HHS avoid responsibility for both the MMR vaccine and, later, Thimerosal's role in the autism epidemic. The "Danish Studies"—six of them in total—would be used to kick out thousands of vaccine-injured claims from Vaccine Court in 2011. One of the cases dismissed was for Grundvig's son."

http://www.theepochtimes.com/n3/2106204-master-ma-nipulator-reveals-how-fraudulent-research-hid-truth-about-autism/?utm_content=bufferaf7a0&utm_medium=social&utm_source=facebook.com&utm_campaign=buffer

Also directly from Robert F. Kennedy, Jr.'s website discussing the use of certain chemicals in vaccines.

The common canard that US autism rates rose after drug makers removed most thimerosal from pediatric vaccines in 2003 is wrong. That same year, CDC added flu shots containing massive doses of thimerosal to the pediatric schedule. As a result, children today can get nearly as much mercury exposure as children did *from all pediatric vaccines combined in the decade prior to 2003. Worse, thimerosal, for the first time, is being given to pregnant women in flu shots. Furthermore, CDC's current autism numbers are for children born in 2002, when kids were still getting thimerosal in their pediatric vaccines. The best science suggests that thimerosal's complete removal from vaccines is likely to prompt a significant decline in autism. For example, a 2013 CDC study in JAMA Pediatrics shows a 33% drop in autism spectrum disorder in Denmark following the 1992 removal of thimerosal from Danish vaccines. That paper is among 37 peer-reviewed studies linking thimerosal to the autism epidemic.*

http://www.robertfkennedyjr.com/vaccines.html#

This is supported with 39 sources he uses to make this statement – (see the website at http://www.robertfkennedyjr.com/articles/thimerosal_autism.html for the complete list).

So maybe just maybe the event of "flow" was not happening fast and furious enough? Maybe it needed a little boost into the culture? Not questioning the nature of vaccines but of the delivery truck. It seems the mercury was the culprit not the actual active agents of the vaccines. Why, with such findings, would vaccinations be allowed to continue before a new delivery system not injurious can be found. I get it, profit - the perpetcual economic model. but do we have to injure people just for profit? Profit would have been there without the injuries. Maybe there was a bigger game afoot?

So maybe the human body and brain was a little more reluctant and a little too strong to fall and capitulate to the needs and desires of this new economic model? Maybe the addiction was not happening fast enough or the reluctance to become an addict to this model was too strong? Maybe the "tulip bulb" was stronger than the manure being shoveled on top of it? Who knows but hopefully we will find out one day.

Enter the world of gaming

A lot of these articles mention gaming as a critical part of their studies. As parents we have all witnessed and in many cases participated in this activity. I am sure many times wincing at what was happening on screen. As with anything moderation is key but peer-pressure is strongly exercised in that space as well. The play dates and the all day/night sessions over friend's houses. The possible guilt we feel by not letting Johnny or Jane take out that group of "Splinter Cell" computer terrorists. So let's take a look at some of the leading gaming and app titles for 2015.

Leading titles in Gaming and App sales in 2015

Below is a quick list from Fortune.com July 2015 as to the leading titles to date for 2015.

The best selling games of the first half of 2015 are as follows:

1. Mortal Kombat X (Publisher: Warner Bros.)

2. Grand Theft Auto V (Publisher: Take-Two Interactive Software)

3. Battlefield Hardline (Publisher: Electronic Arts)

4. Call of Duty: Advanced Warfare (Publisher: Activision)

5. Minecraft (Publisher: Microsoft)

6. Batman: Arkham Knight (Publisher: Warner Bros.)

7. Dying Light (Publisher: Warner Bros.)

8. NBA 2K15 (Publisher: Take-Two Interactive Software)

9. The Witcher 3: Wild Hunt (Publisher: CD Projekt Red)

10. Super Smash Bros. (Publisher: Nintendo)

http://fortune.com/2015/07/23/
top-10-selling-video-games-2015-so-far/

Video games spring back on strong console sales

Worldwide digital video game sales hit a record last year as the mobile market continued to rocket higher and hardcore gamers gravitated toward console downloads.

The market for digital games grew 8 percent from 2014 to $61 billion, according to a new report from gaming intelligence firm SuperData Research.

Downloads to consoles, like Microsoft's Xbox and Sony's PlayStation, saw the biggest jump. Digital console game sales were up 34 percent last year, though the category remained relatively small at $4 billion.

At the same time, software sales at U.S. brick-and-mortar stores continued to fall, slipping 13 percent to $5.3 billion, according to NPD Group.

"Sales figures point toward a shift in the industry as more consumers have adopted digitally distributed games and free-to-play," said SuperData CEO and founder Joost van Dreunen.

The market for tablet and smartphone titles surged 10 percent to $25.1 billion from the previous year.

The mobile space continues to be dominated by a handful of high earners. The top 10 games in the segment accounted for nearly a quarter of total revenue.

http://www.cnbc.com/2015/01/15/video-games-spring-back-on-strong-console-sales.html

Here are the leading App titles for 2015

The list: Top downloads

Top free iPhone apps:

1. Trivia Crack

2. Messenger

3. Dubsmash

4. Instagram

5. Snapchat

6. YouTube

7. Facebook

8. Uber

9. Crossy Road - Endless Arcade Hopper

10. Google Maps

Top paid iPhone apps:

1. Heads Up!

2. Minecraft: Pocket Edition

3. Trivia Crack (Ad Free)

4. Five Nights at Freddy's 2

5. Facetune

6. Geometry Dash

7. Five Nights at Freddy's

8. Afterlight

9. Plague Inc.

10. Goat Simulator

Top free iPad apps:

1. Crossy Road - Endless Arcade Hopper

2. Candy Crush Soda Saga

3. Messenger

4. Netflix

5. YouTube

6. The Calculator - Free

7. Microsoft Word

8. Trivia Crack

9. Skype for iPad

10. Pinterest

Top paid iPad apps:

1. Minecraft: Pocket Edition

2. Five Nights at Freddy's 2

3. Five Nights at Freddy's

4. Geometry Dash

5. Terraria

6. Goat Simulator

7. Heads Up!

8. Five Nights at Freddy's 3

9. Toca Kitchen 2

10. Monument Valley

http://mashable.com/2015/12/09/
apple-best-ios-apps-2015/#wKAOrDCzHPq3

If you notice 50% of these titles, both games and apps, are a little rough – Mortal Kombat, Grand Theft Auto, Five Nights at Freddy's, Call of Duty, Afterlight, plus – SlenderMan, UnderKill, P.T. SilentHell, etc.

Let's do a quick recap on the nature of these games:

Mortal Kombat

Mortal Kombat: Deception is a fighting game developed and published by Midway as the sixth installment of the Mortal Kombat

(MK) series. It was released for the PlayStation 2 and Xbox in October 2004, and for the Nintendo GameCube in March 2005. Mortal Kombat: Deception follows the storyline from the fifth installment, Deadly Alliance. Its story centers on the revival of the Dragon King Onaga, who attempts to conquer the realms featured in the series after defeating the sorcerers Quan Chi and Shang Tsung, the main antagonists in the previous game, and the Thunder God Raiden, defender of Earthrealm. The surviving warriors from the previous titles join forces to confront Onag.

Grand Theft Auto

I have just spent a half-hour planning the perfect heist. I'm going in smart, knocking out the guards and the staff behind the delicate jewelry counters of the store with a carefully placed smoke bomb, and smashing into each cabinet with the butt of a semi-automatic rifle before making my escape on a nearby getaway bike. I'm reducing my cut so I can hire the best hacker to disable the security system, and a skilled gunman to handle crowd control. And yet, despite my best efforts, with one poorly-taken corner on my bike, it all goes wrong. I should be driving down a dank sewer tunnel, sneaking my way under the city to freedom. Instead, I'm here, mowing down wave after wave of police on the city streets, and for the first time while playing a Grand Theft Auto game, I feel immensely guilty about it.

Five Nights at Freddy's

The main character, whose name is later revealed to be Mike Schmidt,[4] has started a job working as a night watch security guard at the restaurant Freddy Fazbear's Pizza.[3][5] A voicemail message left by Mike's predecessor explains that the animatronic animal characters used at the restaurant, Freddy Fazbear, Bonnie, Chica and the disused Foxy, are able to roam freely around it at night, because if they were left off for too long, their servomotors would lock up. He also adds that the animatronics were no longer allowed to roam freely during the day following an incident referred to as the "Bite of '87", which apparently involved the loss of someone's frontal lobe. The employee warns Mike that if one of the robots encounters a human, they will automatically assume that it is an endoskeleton that is not in costume yet, and "forcefully stuff them" into a spare mechanical Freddy Fazbear costume, killing the person in the process.[6]

SlenderMan

The Slender Man (also known as Slenderman) is a fictional super-natural character that originated as an Internet meme created by Something Awful forums user Eric Knudsen (a.k.a. "Victor Surge") in 2009. It is depicted as resembling a thin, unnaturally tall man with a blank and usually featureless face, wearing a black suit.

Stories of the Slender Man commonly feature him stalking, abducting or traumatizing people, particularly children.[1] The Slender Man is not confined to a single narrative, but appears in many disparate works of fiction, mostly composed online.[2] Fiction relating to the Slender Man encompasses many media, including literature, art and video series such as Marble Hornets. Outside of online fiction, the Slender Man has had impact on popular culture, having been referenced in the video game Minecraft and generated video games of his own, such as Slender: The Eight Pages and Slender: The Arrival.

http://www.gamespot.com/reviews/ grand-theft-auto-5-ps4-xbox-one-pc-review/1900-6415959/

So by now I'm sure you are confused and doubting your choices and allowances with respect to how your kids are spending their time. Also be wary of what that time is worth to you, them, and the economic model this is supporting.

But now, let's see what the real price of this meal is?

How much money are the "ranchers" making while your young ones are busy keeping quiet so you can get through your day or two jobs and then – you know, just life stuff?

Chapter 7
Sold off in pieces
Establishing market value

So now that we have the pieces in place, we need to know the price on each section of this valuable veal chop? This is easily done using information that is available online.

Each social network has its own valuation. This is usually based on an average amount of money generated by each user. Valuations on each social network vary greatly but in each case they are talking primarily about one thing – you and your love of this game.

Valuations are typically based on users × revenue generated per user. Example, Facebook has 1.5 billion users worldwide × $24.00 per user equals $36 billion dollar valuation.

So just to have some fun, let's see how much does the average child/adolescent/young adult ages 12 to 25 weigh? Let's just say about 140 pounds so divide 24 by 140 and that's about 17¢ a lb.

So that is how the graphic is made up. Each social network listed or tagged is shown with the price per lb. of each user with the average being 140 pounds. Seems a bit crude and rude but isn't that what works today? Isn't almost every move you make online measured and tagged before you make it? The only way this isn't happening today is when someone like Louie CK releases a show online without making any reference to it through almost any form of media or public relations just to see if it will work without the hype. Very brave move but it seems he wants to see if there is any quality to the work and not just online hype that drives the traffic.

Here are the rest broken down for you using the same metric.

Network	Valuation	Users	Per Lb.
Digg	$164,000,000	10,000,000	0.11¢
Vimeo	$300,000,000	22,000,000	0.09¢
Pinterest	$11,000,000,000	100,000,000	0.78¢
Google+	$15,800,000,000	300,000,000	0.37¢
Twitter	$10,000,000,000	305,000,000	0.23¢
Instagram	$17,500,000,000	400,000,000	0.31¢
YouTube	$40,000,000,000	1,100,000,000	0.25¢
Facebook	$328,000,000,000	1,600,000,000	$1.46

The calculation used is Valuation/Users/140lb. average. Again I know it's a little crass and rude but isn't this what these platforms encourage?

Pretty interesting stuff, no - but hasn't this always happened? According to Paul Simon, "Every generation throw a hero up the pop charts." True, but they usually came into an existing market base and had to compete to win. The Beatles over Elvis – the Rolling Stones over the Beatles (never) then to modern day Kanye over Kanye over Kim over Kanye over Taylor over Kanye.......

Now we even have virtual stars and commodities like...

Japan's holographic rock star -- Miku Hatsune

> *Virtual idol Miku Hatsune has gone from a character marketing voice synthesizing software to a full blown pop star -- pretty clever for a hologram*

> *By Robert Michael Poole 11 November, 2010*

> *Fans collect 3D models of Miku.*

Forget the tantrums, entourage and ridiculous riders. Here's one rock star that only needs electricity to keep her happy.

Following on from Japan's cybernetic pop star, Miku Hatsune has been filling venues in Japan since her first solo live show in March of this year. Originally a character designed to promote Yamaha's vocaloid synthesizing technology -- we all know how Japan loves its characters -- Miku has now taken to the stage and attracts fans in their thousands.

Into a new dimension

Miku Hatsune (literally "future first-sound") debuted on August 31, 2007 at age 16 -- an age she will presumably always remain -- when Crypton Future Media released its first character vocal series software package.

The company decided it didn't only need a cover star for the software, but a character to represent the voice. Her voice was sampled by voice-actress Saki Fujita.

Miku has already been shot into space, when on May 21 this year the Japan Aerospace Exploration Agency launched the Japanese Venus spacecraft explorer Akatsuki.

http://travel.cnn.com/tokyo/play/hologram-484669/

Fabricated stars have been used before to generate revenue. Well for my generation it started with decoder rings in cereal boxes and on the radio but it really hit its height when television arrived in every home in America. Every kid in the 1950s watched and wanted a Davey Crockett raccoon cap.

Davey Crockett was played by Fess Parker was viewed on Sunday nights. It was one of the first appointment television series that came about. It was pretty much a phenomenon.

Coonskin Cap Clings to 'Crockett'

Fess Parker, who rocketed to fame as TV's frontiersman, has found the label hard to escape, even with success in very different ventures.

August 23, 2002|JOHN JOHNSON | TIMES STAFF WRITER

LOS OLIVOS, Calif. — Heavy hangs the coonskin cap.

It's been almost 50 years since Fess Parker donned the fuzzy headgear that launched the first blockbuster cultural phenomenon of the baby boom generation.

At its peak, the frenzy started by Parker's Davy Crockett charac-
ter helped sell 5,000 coonskin caps a day, causing the price of rac-
coon fur to jump from 25 cents a pound to $8. Before it was over,
Crockettmania accounted for $300 million in sales of everything
from Davy wristwatches to lunch boxes.

"I will immodestly tell you it was bigger than anything, ever, in-
cluding The Beatles and Elvis," Parker says in a rumbly Texas
drawl as he cuts into a stack of hot cakes. Dressed in a work shirt
and jeans, he eats breakfast frequently these days at his wine
country inn north of Santa Barbara, where he pursues his second
career as a developer, hotelier and vintner.

http://articles.latimes.com/2002/aug/23/local/me-fess23

That's $300 million in sales in the 1950s – yikes - what is that today ad-
justed for inflation – roughly $2.7 billion! And Parker got none of it – amazing.

In the 1960s the mash-up group – "The Monkees" - Mike Nesmith, Micky Do-
lenz, Peter Tork and the incredibly cute Davy Jones was actually made up to cash
in on the British invasion. Davey was the only Brit but the he was the front man
for the group. Don Kirschner, a major player in the music industry – decided to
come up with a group a see if he could promote the hell out of it. He did and they
did and to this very day, over 50 years later. But, in this mid twentieth century
example the audience wasn't bred or constructed; the group/talent was created
not the desire.

This was all before the famous Nielsen ratings came about. They were the
premier service that measured what was being watched and when on an average in homes across the country. This is still going on today via Google, Facebook
and all the other social media networks throughout the Internet.

What are they interested in? Pretty much the same thing these companies
have always been interested in, how much of the user's spending dollars have
gone to online purchases, games, music and media?

When before has media become a commodity?

The purpose of media has always been to enhance the economy. Take "soap
operas" for example. Their only purpose was to sell cleaning products. The only
reason media has spread the way it has is because of the impetus in generating
advertising sales. As sales dropped, many media platforms: newspapers, magazine, radio and now television are undergoing serious changes. Video killed the
radio star now the Internet is killing the remaining media stars and their vehicles.

But not so fast – many attempts at online video channels even from the traditional networks have been met with failure. MSNBC developed shift.com, part of the MSNBC family and it was shuttered in very little time. This also happened to HuffingtonPost LIVE and Yahoo Screen. With more and more advertising dollars going from traditional to online budgets it is hard to understand these failures except and possibly as a last ditch attempt at keeping the money in the hands of traditional kingdoms.

Early days of television and radio?

There was a similar paradigm in an earlier media transition. Radio sort of killed the newspaper industry but not really. Long form always live on the printed page. But once you had talking, moving images every night for free in your living room – aka television – the game was over.

News and entertainment came into homes in approximately the same size piece of furniture that the radio took up, and there really was no comparison. So video really did kill the radio star and then the television manufacturer tried to kill the television star.

RCA canceling Sid Caesar?

In the early days of television Sid Caesar became its biggest star. His "Show of Shows" had a cadre of writers that would go on to become legends in entertainment: Mel Brooks, Woody Allen, Carl Reiner, Neil Simon, Larry Gelbart, etc.

The really amazing thing about the show was that it was so popular RCA (the show's and NBC's parent company) couldn't keep up with demand for new television sets. So, not to have its competitors eat up a sizeable part of the physical product market, RCA cancelled the NBC Sid Caesar show until it could meet the demand for television sets.

This was how much control the old model gave the corporations still similar today on network but not so true on this new Internet platform.

Future viewing trends

It is never easy figuring out "how they will come at you" like Michael Corleone in the burial scene. But you can always bet "whoever makes the deal for Barzini will be the traitor," so how is the deal for your time and attention being structured for the future?

Well, according to *Forbes* here is a bit of positioning based on the data of how this new generation consumes content.

> What is the trend with regard to cable versus alternate viewing mediums like DVRing, Netflix, and so on? Deloitte notes that households have an average of seven connected devices, and that number will grow over time. The company's Digital Democracy Survey revealed a great deal of relevant data. For example, 37% of U.S. consumers today own the trio of tablets, laptops, and smartphones, a percentage that represents a 270% increase since 2010. In the same timeframe, women have gone from just about 11% of those trio-owners to 45% of those owning all three devices. And a major factor in trends is generational differences, which aren't always obvious when you look at the broad data but which significantly change consumption patterns from one generation to the next.

> http://www.forbes.com/sites/markhughes/2015/03/21/
> the-millennial-trends-that-are-killing-cable/#6c1d75ff4f8f

In the next and final section I hope to offer some insight into all of this and to present some possible solutions.

Chapter 8
Conclusion:
What can be done?

My maternal grandmother raised nine children alone during the Great Depression – the real one. Her two husbands passed and she was left alone with these nine children. She along with her children – seven daughters and two sons – built up a simple grocery/butcher store that stood as the cornerstone of our neighborhood for over 70 years. When my two aunts (who later ran the business after my grandmother) passed themselves, the line at the funeral home stood solid for two straight days. My own parents worked their butts off for years upon years to make sure their kids had a future. They ran our family like our other extended families ran theirs. They were disciplined and still the funniest people you ever met. So anyone thinking I have some contempt for working families is not getting the point. I admire these people both father and mother. My purpose is to open the eyes of hard working people, who try to build families yet are preyed upon by the people who are selected to "protect and serve." That is the motto – the credo – the promise made by all civil servants, elected and appointed.

Let's look at the three components of this "perfect storm" again.

- The marketplace manipulators

- The abusive technologists

- The lack of governance and a societal body

How can we prevent the convergence specifically for our children and their children.

First follow the market manipulators:

- Banks - Mortgage rates and lending practices

- Wall street - stock market

- Media – truth and image

Mortgage rates and lending practices

Low borrowing requirements that were fostered by and empowered very low interest rates on mortgages and home equity loans are obviously the first thing that comes to mind. Just like a gambling addict, you think you can beat the house, but you never can.

Simply be aware, to realize when something comes too easily it probably won't work. When something seems too good to be true – well usually it is. When housing prices appear to get you rich quick (home equity), usually it will have an equal and opposite effect, like putting you in debt.

Wall Street - stock market

This is a rigged game like the "tulip bubble." The best investment advice for generating wealth is to know when to walk away from the table. It is not long term anymore. Short quick buys – in and out – have become brothel behavior – now more than ever. Long term seems to just leave you open to demise and no final reward.

Media – truth and image

Roger Ailes, Rupert Murdoch – need I say more? Also the liberal media has conformed, foolishly I like to believe, in an effort not to bring a knife to a gunfight.

The abusive technologists

Like anything, moderation is the key. This machine as Steve Jobs has said is the bicycle we use to get around the world. His great analogy reminds us that man is not the fastest species on the planet. The cheetah and many others are faster; however, put man on a bicycle and man does become the fastest. Notwithstanding, how many of us have watched as a monkey or bear rides a bicycle in the circus.

Why bring that up? Well, think about it for a second. A monkey or a circus bear rides the bicycle but not really with the intended purpose as people use computers not with the truly intended purpose - not to advance the culture but basically to be distracted from it and to just play around.

Try to measure the use and effectiveness of this technology by the progress and the benefits it has brought us. Do social networks help us? Of course they have, but with good comes bad. It is the proportion that is important. Remember if the 80/20 equation shifts to 20/80 then there is a problem.

But what can be done?

Lots can be done, every day. By educating yourself to the pros and cons you can help your children find and master their way through this maze of information and opportunities.

Here is an edited article concerning use of handhelds for children under 12. For the full version on all of the numbered items please click the link.

10 Reasons Why Handheld Devices Should Be Banned for Children Under the Age of 12

The American Academy of Pediatrics and the Canadian Society of Pediatrics state infants aged 0-2 years should not have any exposure to technology, 3-5 years be restricted to one hour per day, and 6-18 years restricted to 2 hours per day (AAP 2001/13, CPS 2010). Children and youth use 4-5 times the recommended amount of technology, with serious and often life threatening consequences (Kaiser Foundation 2010, Active Healthy Kids Canada 2012). Handheld devices (cell phones, tablets, electronic games) have dramatically increased the accessibility and usage of technology, especially by very young children (Common Sense Media, 2013). As a pediatric occupational therapist, I'm calling on parents, teachers and governments to ban the use of all handheld devices for children under the age of 12 years. Following are 10 research-based reasons for this ban. Please visit zonein.ca to view the Zone'in Fact Sheet for referenced research.

1.Rapid brain growth

2. Delayed Development

3. Epidemic Obesity

4. Sleep Deprivation

5. Mental Illness

6. Aggression

7. Digital dementia

8. Addictions

9. Radiation emission

10. Unsustainable

http://www.huffingtonpost.com/cris-rowan/10-reasons-why-handheld-devices-should-be-banned_b_4899218.html

Listing the abusive use of technologies can go on forever. Most people say that using the technology to its' full potential is up to the user. But is it really?

In a simple sum-up I would argue that people have the right to fair play. The right to a social contract. Think of this analogy; if the only food in the supermarket kills you (pretty much what we have) then is it up to you to create a farm? Or should you trust in the political and societal mechanisms like the FDA? Foolish to do so, really? How do we go forward if you have to do everything or is this where going off the grid becomes a viable stance? Does a society truly function if they don't have the right to expect some form of integrity? Or at least hope that the individuals we position to be in the office of civil servant have our best interests at heart?

The lack of governance and a societal body

The governing and societal body (or lack thereof...) has had a lot of influence in this area overall. Think about it for a second – Net Neutrality – DMCA – FCC – were all of these areas fought over like crazy to structure this for the benefit of a select few? Wasn't our society based on democracy and freedom for all, since its inception, wasn't that meant to generate a level playing field? Or was it only for the meager amount of startups that monopolized the space in the name of standards? Or is it just like the actions of predatory lending mobilized through the oligarchy of banks that is now gone unchecked – were we always "veal" - plain and simple?

All of these events have created ripples that were felt as far as Iceland, where fake loans and share prices drove that country's economy to its knees. This was entwined in a financial web so twisted you can get dizzy just trying to read the article describing the flow of the cash.

It was in this room that some of Iceland's most powerful bankers, executives, and investors had to answer to special investigator Olaf Hauksson. A tall man with a heavy build, Haukkson has spent the past six years investigating the transactions that brought Iceland's economy to its knees in October 2008.

At the time, the country's three biggest banks folded within just three days, in part because their senior executives had illegally doctored the stock listings of their own banks. "Market manipulation", as Hauksson curtly calls it.

When asked what happened to the three bank bosses in the end, Hauksson grins. "They all went to jail," he says, pointing to the empty chairs. "They sat right there."

Olafur Hauksson has only just begun to wrap up proceedings for the biggest scandal in Iceland's history. And it's entirely possible that the publication of the Panama Papers will trigger the next one.

http://panamapapers.sueddeutsche.de/articles/56fec0cda1bb8d3c3495adfc/

So the main difference between Iceland's economic turmoil and the one in the United States is the Icelandic culprits went to jail. A big difference and one that may – just may – cause the problem never to happen again in Iceland – not here.

So back to the previous point - if it is Darwinian within the sphere of abusive technologies, then isn't this where the government – you know the "protect and serve" folks – should oversee what is going on? Even the worst "rancher" knows you have to feed and care for the cows to continue to get milk.

One thing I've learned over the past 30 years of being in this space is that nothing comes to fruition until the money matches the effort. By that I mean until the powers that control the flow of the economy have a strong handle on this new economy, the economy that will obviously change all economies that came before it and fashion all economies after it – nothing seems to go forward. It just gets held back until the damage is too great and any form of pioneer capitulates and conforms to the power structure at hand.

Now apply this to the mortgage industry, the agricultural industry, pharmaceutical, energy, environmental protection services, etc. There seems to be no form of governance once a profit motive or mechanism is involved.

Once you realize this you can see that we have always been "veal," the concept that our children have been bred to drive this new economy and have not been fashioned as we were, driven or corralled, it becomes apparent how these actions of "breeding" are possible. Same moves, same tools just a bit more proactive – not reactive to our choice, not just limiting our choices but, actually breeding them to react selectively to the desired choices.

What can you do to prevent all of this from happening again?

Always go forward by educating yourself every day. How can you educate yourself every day on the advantages and disadvantages of the use of digital technology? This is not an easy task but a doable one. Today, our children – your children - are racing forward into a new world; one that they will live in for the rest of their lives, and every day you have a choice to learn about this new world. Passivity is last century. Interactivity is this new century and this new age. The transition between the two can be exhausting especially when you are carrying the baggage of the last century around with you.

How many qualities and characteristics of this new "Gen-i" are part of your DNA? Are you capable of being truly interactive, isolated, iterative, Internet driven, immaterial, isogonics, isomorphic, (cyber) itinerant, inoculated, etc.? Probably not, but this is the cost of the transition to a time of greater productivity. Right now you laugh and say, "what productivity – Candy Crush?"

Ask yourself if the way you do any of these things has changed:

- Banking
- Communicating
- Entertainment
- Education
- Information
- Purchasing
- Traveling

Have they become easier and cheaper? Have they been impacted by the creation of technology? Have they changed the dynamics of the economic structure? Where are all the workers who used to work the physical components of these jobs? Where have the warehouse staff, the drivers, the loaders-unloaders, the pressmen, forklift operators - found employment?

If you still don't think this was premeditated and orchestrated as part of a new economic model then ask yourself what happens at these global economic summits like G8 and G20? You think these world economic powers don't speculate on what and how these changes will play out? Do you really believe that all of these swings and bubbles are just random acts?

What usually happens when the general population is left with too much time on their hands? What happens when people, families do not have a proper liveable income? Maybe the best control mechanism is fear and borderline poverty?

You can't just shrug and say, "I don't know", if you won't accept these premises as a reason for the decline in the opportunity and optimism. It comes from somewhere and if you have a better idea I would like to hear it.

Send me an email, a tweet, an IM, a SnapChat, an FB private message, a Google chat, call me on What'sApp, Skype, etc., etc., etc.

Bibliography and cited works

"7 Year Old Jurassic World Fan Spends £4,000 of His Father's Money on In-Game Trans-
actions | SegmentNext." SegmentNext 7 Year Old Jurassic World Fan Spends 4000 of
His Fathers Money on InGame Transactions Comments. N.p., 31 Dec. 2015. Web. 22
Aug. 2016. <http://segmentnext.com/2015/12/31/7-year-old-jurassic-world-fan-
spends-4000-of-his-fathers-money-on-in-game-transactions/>.

"Asia Pacific." Japan's Holographic Rock Star. N.p., n.d. Web. 22 Aug. 2016. <http://travel.
cnn.com/tokyo/play/hologram-484669/>.

The Atlantic. Atlantic Media Company, n.d. Web. 22 Aug. 2016.
<http://www.theatlantic.com/education/archive/2015/01/
the-surprising-amount-of-time-kids-spend-looking-at-screens/384737/>.

Bbc.co.uk. N.p., n.d. Web. <http://www.bbc.co.uk/food/food_matters/veal.shtml>.

"Book Review: 'Master Manipulator' Accuses CDC of Manipulating Science on Autism." The Epoch Times Book Review Master Manipulator Accuses CDC of Manipulating Science on Autism Comments. N.p., 04 July 2016. Web. 22 Aug. 2016.
<http://www.theepochtimes.com/n3/2106204-master-manipulator-reveals-how-
fraudulent-research-hid-truth-about-autism/?utm_content=bufferaf7a0&utm_
medium=social&utm_source=facebook.com&utm_campaign=buffer>.

Cieply, Michael, and Brooks Barnes. "Jerry Weintraub, a Force in Film and Music, Dies
at 77." The New York Times. The New York Times, 06 July 2015. Web. 22 Aug. 2016.
<http://www.nytimes.com/2015/07/07/arts/jerry-weintraub-a-force-in-film-and-
music-dies-at-77.html>.

Condliffe, Jamie. "This Kid Blew $2,500 on In-Game Purchases in Just 10 Minutes." Giz-
modo. N.p., 01 Mar. 2013. Web. 22 Aug. 2016.

"Coonskin Cap Clings to 'Crockett'" Los Angeles Times. Los Angeles Times, 23 Aug.
2002. Web. 22 Aug. 2016. <http://articles.latimes.com/2002/aug/23/local/
me-fess23>.

"Creative Destruction." : The Concise Encyclopedia of Economics. N.p., n.d. Web. 22 Aug.
2016. <http://www.econlib.org/library/Enc/CreativeDestruction.html>.

"Data Point: How Many Hours Do Millennials Eat Up a Day?" WSJ. N.p., n.d. Web. 22 Aug. 2016. <http://blogs.wsj.com/digits/2014/03/13/data-point-how-many-hours-do-millennials-eat-up-a-day/?mod=e2tw&mg=blogs-wsj&url=http%3A%2F%2Fblogs.wsj.com%2Fdigits%2F2014%2F03%2F13%2Fdata-point-how-many-hours-do-millennials-eat-up-a-day%3Fmod%3De2tw>.

"Does Too Much Screen Time Make Kids Sick?" Psychology Today. N.p., n.d. Web. 22 Aug. 2016. <https://www.psychologytoday.com/blog/moral-landscapes/201404/does-too-much-screen-time-make-kids-sick>.

"// Encyclopedia." Killer App Definition from PC Magazine Encyclopedia. N.p., n.d. Web. 22 Aug. 2016. <http://www.pcmag.com/encyclopedia/term/45817/killer-app>.

Fetini, Alyssa. "The Keating Five." Time. Time Inc., 08 Oct. 2008. Web. 22 Aug. 2016. <http://content.time.com/time/business/article/0,8599,1848150,00.html>.

Forbes. Forbes Magazine, n.d. Web. 22 Aug. 2016. <http://www.forbes.com/sites/maggiemcgrath/2014/07/31/exxon-mobil-and-conocophillips-in-negative-stock-territory-despite-profit-growth/>.

Forbes. Forbes Magazine, n.d. Web. 22 Aug. 2016. <http://www.forbes.com/sites/markhughes/2015/03/21/the-millennial-trends-that-are-killing-cable/#6c1d75ff4f8f>.

Forbes. Forbes Magazine, n.d. Web. 22 Aug. 2016. <http://www.forbes.com/sites/sageworks/2014/06/15/heres-the-growth-chart-on-day-care-businesses/>.

"The Future of Money in a Mobile Age." Pew Research Center Internet Science Tech RSS. N.p., 17 Apr. 2012. Web. 22 Aug. 2016. <http://www.pewinternet.org/2012/04/17/the-future-of-money-in-a-mobile-age-2/>.

"Gen-i:The Rise of Generation Interactive | OnEnterFrame." OnEnterFrame. N.p., n.d. Web. 22 Aug. 2016. <http://patrickaievoli.com/gen-ithe-rise-of-generation-interactive/>.

Gongloff, Mark. "The Sad State Of America's Middle Class, In 6 Charts." The Huffington Post. TheHuffingtonPost.com, n.d. Web. 22 Aug. 2016. <http://www.huffingtonpost.com/2015/01/20/middle-class-charts_n_6507506.html>.

Goodman, Stephanie. "Robert De Niro Pulls Anti-Vaccine Documentary From Tribeca Film Festival." The New York Times. The New York Times, 26 Mar. 2016. Web. 22 Aug. 2016. <http://www.nytimes.com/2016/03/27/movies/robert-de-niro-pulls-anti-vaccine-documentary-from-tribeca-film-festival.html?_r=0>.

"Grand Theft Auto 5 PS4/Xbox One/PC Review." GameSpot. N.p., n.d. Web. 22 Aug. 2016. <http://www.gamespot.com/reviews/grand-theft-auto-5-ps4-xbox-one-pc-review/1900-6415959/>.

Harden, Seth. "Average Home Sale Price." Statistic Brain. N.p., 29 Feb. 2016. Web. 22 Aug. 2016. <http://www.statisticbrain.com/home-sales-average-price/>.

Hooker, Brian S., "39 published peer reviewed studies linking Thimeresol to Autism," May 30, 2015. <http://www.robertfkennedyjr.com/articles/thimerosal_autism.html>

"Index of /org/InsightBusiness/ib." Index of /org/InsightBusiness/ib. N.p., n.d. Web. 22 Aug. 2016.

"Kanye West Suddenly Realizes In-App Purchases in Kids Games Aren't Cool." Time. Time, n.d. Web. 22 Aug. 2016. <http://time.com/4069228/kanye-west-kim-kardashian-in-app-purchases-games/>.

Klass, Perri. "Fixated by Screens, but Seemingly Nothing Else." The New York Times. The New York Times, 09 May 2011. Web. 22 Aug. 2016. <http://www.nytimes.com/2011/05/10/health/views/10klass.html?_r=0>.

Livingston, Gretchen, and D'Vera Cohn. "U.S. Birth Rate Falls to a Record Low; Decline Is Greatest Among Immigrants." Pew Research Centers Social Demographic Trends Project RSS. N.p., 29 Nov. 2012. Web. 22 Aug. 2016. <http://www.pewsocialtrends.org/2012/11/29/u-s-birth-rate-falls-to-a-record-low-decline-is-greatest-among-immigrants/>.

"Maryland 'free-range' Parents under Fire Again." CNN. Cable News Network, n.d. Web. 22 Aug. 2016. <http://www.cnn.com/2015/04/13/living/feat-maryland-free-range-parenting-family-under-investigation-again/>.

Merriam-Webster. Merriam-Webster, n.d. Web. 22 Aug. 2016.

Morris, Chris. "The Top 10 Selling Video Games of 2015 (so Far)." Fortune The Top 10 Selling Video Games of 2015 so Far Comments. N.p., 22 July 2015. Web. 22 Aug. 2016. <http://fortune.com/2015/07/23/top-10-selling-video-games-2015-so-far/>.

N.p., n.d. Web. 22 Aug. 2016. <https://www.census.gov/population/estimates/nation/popclockest.txt>.

N.p., n.d. Web. <http://onlinelibrary.wiley.com/store/10.1002/asi.21540/asset/21540_ftp.pdf;jsessionid=FA974B8577892FA504E148E0F668BF8C.f02t03?v=1&t=ihmnczuu&s=1f9e5fc89333856a020829027a55f771fea59658>.

N.p., n.d. Web. <https://www.linkedin.com/pulse/just-say-patrick-aievoli?trk=mp-author-card>.

N.p., n.d. Web. <http://www.iab.net/wiki/print/>.

N.p., n.d. Web. <http://www.ncbi.nlm.nih.gov/pmc/articles/PMC284>.

N.p., n.d. Web. <http://www.statisticbrain.com/home-sales-average-price/>.

"Online Activities." Pew Research Center Internet Science Tech RSS. N.p., 15 Dec. 2010. Web. 22 Aug. 2016. <http://www.pewinternet.org/2010/12/16/online-activities/>.

"Panama Papers: A Storm Is Coming to Iceland." Süddeutsche.de. N.p., n.d. Web. 22 Aug. 2016. <http://panamapapers.sueddeutsche.de/articles/56fec0cda1bb8d3c3495adfc/>.

Pappas, Stephanie. "Social Media Cyber Bullying Linked to Teen Depression." Scientific American. N.p., n.d. Web. 22 Aug. 2016. <http://www.scientificamerican.com/article/social-media-cyber-bullying-linked-to-teen-depression/>.

Perez, Sarah. "Apple's App Store Saw $1.7B in Billings And Broke Customer Records In July." TechCrunch. N.p., 07 Aug. 2015. Web. 22 Aug. 2016.

"Petroleum Technology History Part 1 - Background - Greatest Engineering Achievements of the Twentieth Century." Petroleum Technology History Part 1 - Background - Greatest Engineering Achievements of the Twentieth Century. N.p., n.d. Web. 22 Aug. 2016. <http://www.greatachievements.org/?id=3677>.

Rajewski, Jonathan. "How to Avoid Becoming a Victim of a 'Catfish'" The Huffington Post. TheHuffingtonPost.com, n.d. Web. 22 Aug. 2016. <http://www.huffingtonpost.com/jonathan-rajewski/how-to-avoid-becoming-a-v_1_b_2507220.html>.

"Remembering EWorld, Apple's Forgotten Online Service." Macworld. N.p., n.d. Web. 22 Aug. 2016. <http://www.macworld.com/article/2202091/remembering-eworld-apples-forgotten-online-service.html>.

"Robert F. Kennedy Jr." Robert F. Kennedy Jr. N.p., n.d. Web. 22 Aug. 2016. <http://www.robertfkennedyjr.com/vaccines.html#>.

Rowan, Cris. "10 Reasons Why Handheld Devices Should Be Banned for Children Under the Age of 12." The Huffington Post. TheHuffingtonPost.com, n.d. Web. 22 Aug. 2016. <http://www.huffingtonpost.com/cris-rowan/10-reasons-why-handheld-devices-should-be-banned_b_4899218.html>.

"RTDNA - Radio Television Digital News Association." RTDNA. N.p., n.d. Web. 22 Aug. 2016.

"Supply and Demand: Basic Economics Part 2." Supply and Demand: Basic Economics Part 2. N.p., n.d. Web. 22 Aug. 2016. <http://www.socialstudiesforkids.com/articles/economics/supplyanddemand2.htm>.

The Telegraph. Telegraph Media Group, n.d. Web. 22 Aug. 2016. <http://www.telegraph.co.uk/news/2016/04/13/robert-de-niro-there-is-a-link-between-vaccines-and-autism/>.

Titcomb, James. "Apple Reports Biggest Annual Profit in History with Net Income of $53.4bn." The Telegraph. Telegraph Media Group, n.d. Web. 22 Aug. 2016. <http://www.telegraph.co.uk/technology/apple/11959016/Apple-reports-biggest-annual-profit-in-history.html>.

"University of Michigan Health System." Television (TV) and Children: Your Child:. N.p., n.d. Web. 22 Aug. 2016. <http://www.med.umich.edu/yourchild/topics/tv.htm>.

US News. U.S.News & World Report, n.d. Web. 22 Aug. 2016. <http://www.us-news.com/opinion/blogs/robert-schlesinger/articles/2016-01-05/us-population-in-2016-according-to-census-estimates-322-762-018>.

"Video Game Use in Boys With Autism Spectrum Disorder, ADHD, or Typical Development." Pediatrics 132.2 (2013): n. pag. Web.

"Video Games Spring Back on Strong Console Sales." CNBC. N.p., 15 Jan. 2015. Web. 22 Aug. 2016. <http://www.cnbc.com/2015/01/15/video-games-spring-back-on-strong-console-sales.html>.

Warren, Christina. "Apple Names the Best IOS Apps of 2015." Mashable. N.p., 09 Dec. 2015. Web. 22 Aug. 2016. <http://mashable.com/2015/12/09/apple-best-ios-apps-2015/#wKAOrDCzHPq3>.

Warren, Christina. "Apple Names the Best IOS Apps of 2015." Mashable. N.p., 09 Dec. 2015. Web. 22 Aug. 2016. <http://mashable.com/2015/12/09/apple-best-ios-apps-2015/#wKAOrDCzHPq3>.

"Was Tulipmania Irrational?" The Economist. The Economist Newspaper, 04 Oct. 2013. Web. 22 Aug. 2016. <http://www.economist.com/blogs/freeexchange/2013/10/economic-history>.

Wikipedia. Wikimedia Foundation, n.d. Web. 22 Aug. 2016. <https://en.wikipedia.org/wiki/Game_Boy#cite_note-10>.

"The World Is Flat." Wikipedia. Wikimedia Foundation, n.d. Web. 22 Aug. 2016. <https://en.wikipedia.org/wiki/The_World_Is_Flat>.

About the author

Patrick Aievoli started his career in 1978 as a designer for local editorial and advertising companies. In 1984, he became a promotional designer at McGraw-Hill.

Professor Aievoli has been a full-time academic since 1989 when he left his position as senior designer, print promotion, at the McGraw-Hill Book Company. During his time at McGraw-Hill Patrick helped in the creation of McGraw-Hill's first interactive CD-ROM "Encyclopedia of Science and Technology" in 1987.

In 1989 Prof. Aievoli started teaching full-time at SUNY Farmingdale immediately starting courses in multimedia. From 1990 to 1996 Prof. Aievoli completed his thesis on "The Use of New Media in Higher Education" culminating in an interactive art history CD-ROM featuring core and dynamic content along with a simplified suite of online learning tools.

In 1998 he became a full-time faculty member at LIU Post in Brookville, NY. He became the director of the campus' Interactive Multimedia Arts graduate program in 1999 and has built the program since the start.

Although he is a dedicated academic, Professor Aievoli is still involved in the new media arena and has consulted for some of the metro area's largest new media companies.

Academic Experience

Associate Professor
Director of the Interactive Multimedia Arts graduate program
Long Island University Post campus
Brookville, New York.

Teaching full time at the college level for the past 27 years, responsible for hiring, budget, recruitment, promotion, technology and advisement.

Course development and teaching experience;
- Interactive design/ Digital imaging – Adobe Creative Suite,
- Digital video/audio – Final Cut/Premiere/After Effects
- Served on curriculum development committee and search committee – Digital Game Design - LIU Post
- USDAN Summer Arts – developed game design program

Client Roster (Partial)

Directly involved in the conception, creation and final production of numerous new media projects for companies:
- American Express
- Association for Computing Machinery
- Autism Academy
- Electro Dynamics, Inc.
- FleetBoston
- LinuxIDG
- McGraw-Hill Health Professions
- New York Islanders
- Verizon/NYNEX
- TimeWarner/SONY
- Tommy Hilfiger USA

Awards

- Long Island Business News – "50 over 50" - 2010
- 6 Time Long Island Advertising Club - Advisor for Student Best On Long Island winner 2002, 2003, 2004, 2006, 2008 and 2009
- How Magazine Award – 1996

Publications

The Digital Incunabula: rock • paper • pixels
2015, Zea Books
Lincoln, Nebraska

"on enterFrame"
2008, Whittier Publications,
Long Beach, NY

"Supporting the Aesthetic through Metaphorical Thinking"
Journal of National Collegiate Honors Council, 4:1 (Fall/Winter 2003),
    pp 89-99,

Colliding Forces, chapter "Collide",
2004, McNabb and Kremer,
Kendall Hunt
Dubuque, Iowa

Presentations

- Seybold Seminars, 1996, 1997, 2000, 2002
- Acxiom Direct Marketing conference, 1999
- CD ROM Live - 1995
- Adobe Event - 1995

Adjudication

- Knowledge Industry Publications (KIP) Top 100 Multimedia Producers 1999-2000
- Long Island Media Arts Juried Exhibition 1999-20